SOUTHERN LITERARY STUDIES

The University of North Carolina Press
Chapel Hill, N. C.

The Baker and Taylor Co.
New York

Oxford University Press
London

Maruzen-Kabushiki-Kaisha
Tokyo

SOUTHERN LITERARY STUDIES
A COLLECTION OF LITERARY, BIO-
GRAPHICAL, AND OTHER SKETCHES, BY
C. ALPHONSO SMITH, WITH A BIOGRAPH-
ICAL STUDY BY F. STRINGFELLOW BARR

CHAPEL HILL
THE UNIVERSITY OF NORTH CAROLINA PRESS
1927

COPYRIGHT 1927, BY

THE UNIVERSITY OF NORTH CAROLINA PRESS

EDWARDS & BROUGHTON COMPANY
RALEIGH, N. C.
United States of America

CONTENTS

I.	C. Alphonso Smith	1
II.	Americanism of American Literature	20
III.	Literature in the South	44
IV.	Historical Tendencies in Recent Southern Literature	71
V.	Southern Oratory Before the War	83
VI.	Thomas Jefferson	94
VII.	Edgar Allan Poe	120
VIII.	Joel Chandler Harris	128
IX.	O. Henry	158
X.	Matthew Fontaine Maury	168
XI.	Bibliography of C. Alphonso Smith	182

SOUTHERN LITERARY STUDIES

One who never turned his back but marched breast forward,
  Never doubted clouds would break,
Never dreamed, though right were worsted, wrong would
    triumph,
Held we fall to rise, are baffled to fight better,
  Sleep to wake.

No, at noonday in the bustle of man's work-time
  Greet the unseen with a cheer!
Bid him forward, breast and back as either should be,
"Strive and thrive!" cry "Speed,—fight on, fare ever
    There as here!"

—Browning.

C. ALPHONSO SMITH

"All things had to be done by Caesar at one time."

THIS sketch must be preceded by an apology. I find it more than difficult to memorialize here the life of Alphonso Smith, for two reasons. First, being of a far younger generation, I feel inadequate to the task of telling what part he played in the development of Southern democracy since the Civil War. Secondly, I distrust my ability to portray his amazing force and his great generosity of spirit, if only because I was so devoted to him during his lifetime. In short, I know too little and perhaps feel too much. Of course there is in front of me, as I write, a formidable mass of material about his life before I knew him or could have known him. But this represents very largely the opinion of others and I must content myself with the barest sketch of dates and facts. To these, I should like to add how it felt to be taught by him in his riper years.

These "documents"! I never before tried to outline the life of a man whom I personally loved. But what can these papers tell, even those which are covered with his characteristic script, penciled, flowing, of a man with the vigor of Alphonso Smith? Only those of my readers who came under the spell of his personality can ever know the measure of my failure.

Suppose I tell first what I have tried to learn from others. It will be brief. On May 28, 1864, in the last eventful year of the war for Southern independence, Dr. J. Henry Smith, pastor of the Presbyterian church in Greensboro, North Carolina, and his wife, Mary Kelly Watson, were given a son. The boy was named Charles Alphonso, for two uncles who had died for the South. J. Henry Smith had been born in Lexington, Virginia, and had been educated at Washington College, now Washington and Lee University with one of J. Henry Smith's sons for president. His wife was the daughter of Judge Egbert Watson of Charlottesville, Virginia.

He must have been a darling little boy, this small fellow growing up in a sleepy Carolina town with his background of Virginia Presbyterianism to lend him a charming seriousness. I knew his own son when he was a tiny lad, and as they were humorously alike, I find it easy to visualize Alphonso in his boyhood home. Besides, at my elbow is a paper scribbled by him when he was nearly fifty-eight, suggesting—though just barely—his earliest recollections. His very earliest seems to have been his putting on his first trousers. And then, when he was six, this little Presbyterian said over and over "I'm six years old," so that the truth side of the ledger kept by God might overbalance the lie side. Not that he was then or ever introspective; I think it was rather an act of wise provision and robust cheerful faith.

He read *Tim the Scissors Grinder* for his first book.

"Once there was a little turkey," recited Alphonso at one of those inevitable child recitals that graced the extreme youth of all of us Americans. "Once there was a little turkey," he repeated, and seems never to have gotten beyond the little turkey's bare existence. For a man who was to be a noted orator himself and to admire and study oratory, Alphonso with his little turkey made an exceedingly poor start. But when his father later rebuked him for his stage fright and for his repeating in varying tones of anguish "Once there was a little turkey," his mother, gentle soul, remarked to his infinite relief: "True, he didn't say it all, but what he did say, he said with a great deal of expression."

"Once there was a little muskrat" would have been a more appropriate remark for Alphonso. He caught them and caught them; and since money was scarce in the Reconstruction South, he netted "ten cents a tail" for them. Once he caught a wildcat, which was more exciting. He wanted to shoot straight with his sling-shot, straight enough to hit a car window in a moving train; and he did manage to do just that, so well that he smashed the window. In his bird-egg collecting, he came off less well: one Jack Dillard sold him some hawk eggs. This was rather thrilling, till Alphonso washed them, and found that ink-spots on pigeon eggs cannot stand washing. But he admired Jack for the way he recited poetry, and ran off and learned pages himself. His father tested his children's chest expansion by seeing how much of the participial portion of Southey's *Lodore* they could recite without drawing breath, thus serving literature and hygiene in one choice gesture.

But school, so far anyhow as Latin was concerned, remained for him a sorry substitute for muskrats till one day his father made a convert. He was helping Alphonso with his Latin. "This is a grand chapter," said his father, and began to translate: " 'All things had to be done by Caesar at one time.' " Into Alphonso's imagination there broke the dauntless, active, driving Roman, in the midst of hostile Gaul. Not only had he so many, many things to do, but—and this is what seems to have stuck in Alphonso's mind through life—*All things had to be done at one time.*

In Greensboro public schools and with his father's aid Alphonso prepared for Davidson College. His brothers, Harry and Egbert, had each led his class there; and Alphonso wondered if he would do as much. Pondering this the night before his final departure for college, Alphonso went out behind the barn and wrestled with his timorous apprehension that he would not uphold his family name.

In Greensboro also he knew the drug clerk, Will Porter, whose biographer one day he was to be when Will was known throughout the civilized world as O. Henry. They camped together and they belonged to the same Serenading Club: Alphonso played the guitar, but Will played "a silent tenor violin."

At Davidson, Alphonso graduated with honor in 1884. Also he won two medals for an essay,—an attack on the atheistic interpretation of the—to him, true—theory of evolution, which he signed: "Teleologist." When his double victory was announced, his class-mates bore him triumphantly on their shoulders. Obviously this was in the pre-stadium days of the American college. Winning these two medals decided him to make the study of English his life work.

There followed four years of school-teaching in two little Carolina towns, Selma and Sanford. He was a personage now, perhaps for the first time. He was called on by country-store debaters to say whether Shakespeare was a man or "just a book like the Bible." He must have learned in these years some of the love he always showed for common humanity. Life in those tiny American towns was intimate: one of his acquaintances knew who had gone where by reading the footprints of his friends in the dirt streets. Meanwhile young Alphonso Smith read much, and continued to commit vast stretches of poetry to memory—Swinburne, Shelley, Poe, Tennyson, Browning. He used to say half-jokingly that he could quote Shakespeare for two hours without stopping. The only time he was challenged, he had to be stopped artificially as it were. Literature in those tiny American towns could be intimate too.

In 1889 he entered Johns Hopkins University as a graduate student in English, history, and German. While he studied, he instructed in English. In 1893 he took his doctorate.

For nine years he taught in Louisiana State University at Baton Rouge. In the summers he ordinarily went home to Greensboro to be with his family, for family ties always meant much to him, or bicycled in Europe with his brothers. During a sabbatical year, he studied at the Sorbonne and in Germany. And it was at Baton Rouge that he produced his first two books. When he left Louisiana to teach in the University of his own State of North Carolina he was asked to address the Louisiana State Legislature—a compliment to his growing powers as a popular speaker. The address he delivered, "Southern Oratory before the War," he repeated on many later occasions. The days of the "little turkey" were gone.

He returned to North Carolina in 1902; three years later he married. His bride was Miss Susie McGee

Heck, of Raleigh, North Carolina. Their three children—the three children I played with a few years later—were born while their father was still at Chapel Hill.

Throughout his life his generous nature found its chief outlet in his wife and children. With the children he played, sang, told stories, fished and trapped. With his wife he read his manuscript when it was fresh from his pen, shared his ambitions and his triumphs. He always rejoiced in his household and sought his deepest happiness at his hearth. "God be thanked," he used to quote from his own and his wife's favorite poet, Robert Browning, "the meanest of his creatures, Boasts two soul sides, one to face the world with, One to show a woman when he loves her."

In 1909 he accepted a call to be the first Edgar Allan Poe Professor of English at the University of Virginia, and simultaneously an appointment as Roosevelt Exchange Professor at the University of Berlin for 1910-11.

Out of old newspaper clippings I have tried to reconstruct for myself that triumph at Berlin: his *Antrittsrede*, the Kaiser and Kaiserin listening; the congratulations and flattering attentions of the Kaiser; the prestige those attentions brought him with the German public and the German press. His visit synchronized with the Centennial Celebration of the University of Berlin, and derived from it added luster.

Back in Virginia he worked, and wrote, and lectured. And since it is "back in Virginia" that I knew him, I feel on surer ground. I was not lucky enough to hear Alphonso recite—with a great deal of expression—the hesitant tale of the little turkey; and I did not see him borne in triumph when he won his medals as a senior at Davidson. Berlin reads to me, as I finger my material, like a patch from a novel of pre-War Germany. But once I can get Alphonso in his home on East Lawn, "back in Virginia," I feel I know my man. I begin to want to call him Dr. Smith again. Yet, since I, like other students of his, called him Alphonso behind his back, in the well-known manner of students, perhaps he would not mind remaining Alphonso here in these pages.

In my mind's eye I see him walking down the lovely Lawn towards Cabell Hall, a big broad-shouldered, slightly stooped man; and I think that my youthful eye was particularly struck by the rear end of his bald patch that peeped from underneath the back brim of his hat. I thought he had rather a majestically ponderous walk.

Or a certain January afternoon in his spacious study, looking out on the Rotunda. I had just heard, during my Christmas vacation in New Orleans, an address by William Lyon Phelps, and was delighted with some of his funny stories. Knowing Alphonso liked funny stories as the very meat and drink of life, I was running them off. When I started to go, already feeling I had usurped time that belonged by rights to things I scarcely understood, he made a gesture of restraint; and with his huge frame shaken by silent mirth, kept murmuring "Tell some more!" John Butler Yeats, the painter, and father of the poet, told me once, "There's wisdom in jokes." Alphonso would have agreed.

He was a superb raconteur himself, and had a particular knack with negro stories. I remember there was a negro preacher, somewhat given to exaggeration—and Alphonso fundamentally liked exaggeration—who wished to tell his congregation just how hot hell was. He recalled to his gaping listeners the molten metal ladled out at foundries. "Well," he concluded, "down in hell dey uses dat stuff fo' ice-cream." Then there was the other preacher who was making an exegesis on the phrase in the parable of the prodigal son: he "came to himself" and arose and went to his father. According to this divine's contention, the prodigal son got so down on his luck that he first pawned his coat, then his vest—the reader can continue the enumeration for himself—until finally he "came to himself" and in this totally denuded state he arose and went to his father. Alphonso loved that story and often used it to illustrate how the mind misunderstands and reads into phrases meanings never there before.

But negroes were not mere buffoons to him, as they are sometimes even to Southerners, who should know better. Aware of their profoundly spiritual qualities of love and gentleness, he interested himself in them beyond jokes. More than once he talked to them in the Colored Baptist Church just down Main Street, below the Union Station, the one with the funny little white steeple. And they loved him and respected him, as they do those who understand them and help them. I doubt if, listening to him in that church, they knew he sang their songs to his own guitar accompaniment when he was alone with his family, and even—would I might have seen it!—clog-danced on occasion.

He was genuinely musical; he not only played his guitar avidly, but he composed for his own pleasure. Chiefly, his music was to be of value to him when he turned to the activity for which in the long run he may be best remembered, I mean the English and Scottish ballads he collected. Many a student at the University Summer School, now teaching in some remote little Southern town, will carry as her chief recollection of him: Alphonso Smith standing on the steps of the Rotunda, his arms round his three little children, and all four lustily singing "Barbara Allen" or some other of his favorites.

Those children were his chief delight. He played with them, told them stories, and sang to them. And with the little boy, like his father called "Phon," he trapped rabbits. But since rabbits are so temperamental about getting into little boys' traps, particularly the first night out, and as little boys cannot be expected to show infinite patience, Alphonso Senior bought some rabbits and put them in Alphonso Junior's traps. I understand that after that, the rabbits rather got the habit.

Have I done wrongly in talking so much of Alphonso Smith's personality and daily life and so little of his intellectual achievements? I seem to hear a reader saying, "After all, this book I have in my hand was gotten out not because Alphonso Smith was personally charming, but because he left his mark on the intellectual life of this nation and achieved great eminence in his chosen profession." I cannot find it in me to apologize. In the first place, I know of no better reason to get out a book of this sort than that its author was known and loved *for himself* as a human being by thousands of readers. In the second place, I am better fitted to deal with the man than with his intellectual contribution. In the third place, every reader of this sketch can by going to the numerous works of Alphonso Smith make his own judgment, while he cannot go to Alphonso Smith whom it was my good fortune to know. And finally, let me be frank about it, I regard his personality as more important than his work.

That does not mean that I have not been an eager reader of his or that I have not derived great inspiration from his teaching. But the side of him that gave me that inspiration was his personal enthusiasm. I believe Alphonso's method of inspiring in his pupils a love of good literature was the simplest and certainly for most pupils the surest method known. He made the student *like* him—him, Alphonso Smith—by the force of his personality. He then demonstrated to the student his own love of literature. And the student, even if literature had always seemed cold and inaccessible, was driven to suspect there was something in it *since Alphonso Smith loved it.*

Whether it was the music of Poe's verse, or the moodiness of Hamlet, or the naïve charm of Chaucer, or the dramatic force of Browning; whether it was the wistfulness of a ballad like "Sir Patrick Spens" or the curious pleasure he always felt in the mere grouping of words, he knew how to communicate his enthusiasm. Maybe a teacher can accomplish no higher task.

I go further than this: I think that those who think of Alphonso Smith as primarily a great "scholar" do both the word and Alphonso Smith an injustice. It was not in analysis or criticism that he left his mark, but in appreciation and in preaching the gospel of his own enthusiasms. But above all he was what I am convinced few analytical or critical minds can ever be, a democrat of deep and lasting faith.

It is as a democrat that I wish to describe him in concluding this brief glimpse of him. He had the genuine crowd-sense that made him a skillful orator. He had the flair for headline titles that the analyst distrusts: "Pinnacle Moments," "Keynote Studies in Keynote Books of the Bible." I do not believe he derived his instinct for headlines from the newspaper; he and the newspaper both derived headlines from the same instinct—an instinct for crowd-thought. He was essentially dramatic; and that, every popular leader must be. He liked the common things of life, common experiences, common sufferings—as his friend O. Henry did too. He yearned to the "four million." And it was because he yearned deeply; because, as my own vulgar generation puts it, he was "sold on" progress, education, democracy, that the people knew him for their own. He was permitted to speak to them intelligently because he felt essentially what they felt. He stood for "applied literature" as Martin Luther stood for "applied religion," neither man being a mystic, and both men putting human life before the idea. Literature must be made applicable to the life and experience of as many men and women as possible. Putting himself in the shoes of the miscellaneous people he met on the streets he walked, in the trains he traveled in, in the cities he visited, he asked of this new self he had created out of Demos: "What can literature do for me?" And he made his question the title of the book by which he is known from one end of America to another. He brought literature down to earth; and he had the faith to believe he had done well.

That faith of his! He had faith in the worthwhileness of life. Therefore great ambition, boundless energy, a zest for the competitive effort that is the breath of democracy, and a respect for the solid success that is its goal, were his. In his teaching he exuded common sense. The same thing that made him a staunch defender of colloquialism and an ardent student of slang; the thing that made him seek constantly the effective, the telling phrase, made him envisage his last work, when he was head of the English Department at Annapolis, as a matter primarily of teaching midshipmen to make reports clear enough to be read. The thing that made him seek the live, the growing forces in life, made him turn to democracy and literacy as the salvation of the South. Far from being a "professional Southerner," he accepted the democratic conceptions against which the South had fought. And he accepted Americanism, not through mere necessity, but with his usual enthusiasm: Americanism was "the greatest ism he knew."

His enthusiasm brought with it an inevitable naïveté that was perhaps not the least of his charms. The same little boy that bought those hawk eggs from Jack Dillard wrote me when he was in his fifties that he had taken a vote in his classes at the Naval Academy to see what author the midshipmen preferred above all others for a ship's library, and that they had overwhelmingly voted for O. Henry. Now, I do not doubt that midshipmen like and will always like O. Henry; but nobody that knows the wicked ways of young men in classes can pass that vote by without a smile. All I care to observe is, the middies not only knew their author, they knew their teacher. Or again, I recall his telling a class in Cabell Hall that he had always regretted reading Boccaccio, because of the filth in his *Decameron*. "Don't read it, gentlemen. It's foul stuff." And the gentlemen dashed from that classroom for the library in a mad race to read Boccaccio from cover to cover. I wonder if the librarian ever guessed what innocent remark started that famous stampede on Boccaccio? But those two instances could be matched by thousands in which he read his audience like an open book.

It was the democratic leader in Alphonso Smith who accepted in 1917 a call to the Chair of English at the United States Naval Academy. He saw in this new field an unrivalled opportunity to send out his students all over the world as ambassadors of American literature. His Americanism was stirred at the thought that his students represented every single state in the Union, as O. Henry's was stirred by the thought that comedy and tragedy could occur in every single city.

In 1924 a sudden illness came on him. The midshipmen whom he loved and who had come to love him in return and look to him as to an older brother, were just leaving for their summer cruise. Alphonso Smith sent them this message: "Tell them that I am not afraid to die. I greet the Unseen with a cheer." He died June 13. For many years he had asked that at his funeral a negro quartet might sing one of his favorite songs, "Swing Low, Sweet Chariot." He repeated his request a few days before his death in a way that left no doubt as to his seriousness. In spite of foolish protests, his family had the wisdom to insist that this last characteristic request of his be obeyed.

He lived a busy, happy life, and died full of honors. He tasted a full measure of success, and of a sort that he respected. He opened the door to literature for thousands of other human beings. He never ceased to enter through that door a garden of delights. Above all, books never usurped the place of life for him; they were always a means of understanding life more fully. He had the widest sympathies. He knew what he called "the glory of the commonplace."

In his youth at Davidson he had been borne on the shoulders of his classmates for his attainments in writing. Throughout life he was borne on the shoulders of his friends; for he felt the constant support of their affection and admiration.

I have not felt it necessary to speak at length of his bulky writings; his writings are more accessible to the world than his personality, and I have wished to speak chiefly of that. But his faith in the importance of his task, his eager zest for life, his tremendous purposefulness enabled him to accomplish an amazing amount of writing on the most varied topics. And he must have felt often enough, like Caesar, that all things had to be done by him at one time. But life contained for him not only work; it contained much friendship, much joy, much laughter. He accomplished his task in this world cheerfully and courageously; and cheerfully and courageously he went to his task in the next. And his courage shall be a token to us when our own courage flags.

F. STRINGFELLOW BARR.

IMPORTANT DATES IN THE LIFE OF
CHARLES ALPHONSO SMITH

Born at 357 Church Street, Greensboro, North Carolina, May 28, 1864.

Prepared for college in public schools of Greensboro. A.B. Davidson College, North Carolina, 1884. A.M. Davidson College, 1887.

Taught in schools at Sanford, Princeton, and Selma, North Carolina, 1884-1889.

Instructor in English, Johns Hopkins University, Baltimore, Md., 1890-1893.

Received Ph.D. degree from Johns Hopkins University, 1893.

Professor of Language and Literature, Louisiana State University, Baton Rouge, 1893-1902.

Studied at the Sorbonne, Paris, and University of Berlin. Research work in British Museum, 1900-1901.

Professor of English Language, University of North Carolina, Chapel Hill, N. C., 1902-1907. Head of English Department, 1907-1909. Dean of Graduate Department, 1903-1909 Founder of *Studies in Philology*.

Married Susie McGee Heck, Raleigh, North Carolina, November 8, 1905. The children of this marriage are:
>Sue Gee Smith.
>Fannie Watson Smith.
>Charles Alphonso Smith, Jr.

Edgar Allan Poe Professor of English, University of Virginia, Charlottesville, Virginia, 1909-1917.

Leave of absence to serve as Roosevelt Professor of American History and Institutions at the University of Berlin, Germany, 1910-1911.

Lecturer at University of California, University of Kansas, Cincinnati University, Chautauqua, Brooklyn Institute of

C. ALPHONSO SMITH 19

Arts and Sciences, Summer School of South, Winthrop College, Union Theological Seminary, etc.

Head of Department of English, United States Naval Academy, Annapolis, Maryland, 1917-1924.

Appointed Lecturer at Military Camps by the Secretary of State of the United States.

Died at 3 Porter Road, United States Naval Academy, June 13, 1924. Buried in Green Hill Cemetery, Greensboro, North Carolina, June 15, 1924.

THE AMERICANISM OF AMERICAN LITERATURE [1]

I AM GOING to speak for a little while this morning on a theme that concerns each one of us by reason of our Americanism. However else we may differ we stand here upon the same platform: we are all Americans, and we are all influenced by and in turn exert influence upon this intangible but irrepressible force that we call Americanism. If I do not mistake the signs of the time, Americanism is the most interesting *ism* that men are now studying. It is unquestionably the greatest word and the most potent idea that our nation has given to history. It sums up our past, it interprets our present, and it prophesies our future.

I shall approach it through our literature. Strange to say it has been approached almost invariably through our political and industrial activities, not through our literary activities. It has been assumed that the American spirit has manifested itself distinctively only in the combined realm of political and industrial captaincy, and that if Americanism cannot be found here, it cannot be found anywhere. This is a superficial view, a view not borne out by the facts.

[1] An address delivered on University Day, October 12, 1911, before the students and faculty of the University of North Carolina.

AMERICANISM OF AMERICAN LITERATURE 21

The Americans who are best known abroad have for a hundred years been our writers, not our statesmen or millionaires. With the exception of Washington, Franklin, Jefferson, and Lincoln, we have had no statesmen and certainly no financiers who could compare for a moment in world renown with Washington Irving, James Fenimore Cooper, Edgar Allan Poe, Henry Wadsworth Longfellow, Ralph Waldo Emerson, Bret Harte, and Mark Twain. These are the men who embody the national spirit and stand as its exponents.

I shall not attempt, however, to study Americanism by citing American authors or American books or American themes of my own choosing. On the contrary, I prefer to take those aspects of American literature that foreigners have themselves found most interesting and most representative and then try to interpret their preferences in terms of a distinctive Americanism. These aspects seem to me to be four. I shall enumerate them separately and then attempt to interpret them.

The first revelation that came to me as I lectured on American literature at the University of Berlin and talked with German men and women about American literature was the significant part that the Indian has played in turning the thoughts of other lands to our own land. I had always thought that it was Washington Irving and his *Sketch Book* that gave American literature a standing abroad. But this is only partly true. Irving introduced American literature into England, but it was Cooper and his Indians that gave American literature standing and vogue on the continent. It is the fashion today to make merry over Cooper. Mark Twain has said that the Leatherstocking Series ought to have been called the "Breaking Twig" Series, because every time something interesting is about to happen, somebody breaks a twig and the intended victim gets away. He finds Cooper's novels strewn with broken twigs. However this may be, Cooper's popularity in Europe remains greater than that of any other American writer. A large class of German university students, that professed utter ignorance of Walt Whitman, had not a man or woman in it that did not know the works of Cooper. His Majesty himself grew enthusiastic at the mention of Cooper's name. "I have read," he said, "everything that Cooper wrote. As a boy I used to sleep with his works under my pillow. I read them in English, too, not in a translation. Cooper is unsurpassed in his larger out-of-doors effects, in his scenes sketched on a broad canvas. He is weak only in minor details."

As fast as Cooper's novels were written they were republished in thirty-four European cities. It is probable, as Bryant says, that no other author ever enjoyed so great a popularity during his own life time. Balzac said that if Cooper had succeeded as well in the portrayal of character as in the portrayal of the phenomena of nature, "he would have uttered the last word of our art." Ruskin said that nobody but Cooper knew how to describe accurately the changing phenomena of sea-foam during a storm.

But it was through his familiarity with pioneer life and especially through his portrayal of Indian character that Cooper made and retains his fame abroad. Scott had already reproduced a brilliant array of characters from the most varied periods of English and continental history; Dickens was about to sketch as only he could the lower classes of English society; George Eliot the middle classes, and Thackeray the higher classes; but these were in a way familiar. The Red Man was original beyond any of them. He came, too, at a time when the cry, "Back to Nature," resounded from every part of Europe. Here was a figure that seemed to embody in an unimagined way the new ideal. He had always lived close to nature. He had few laws, but what he had he obeyed. He was untroubled and unfettered by institutions social, civil, or religious. His antiquity was as vast as that of the Asiatic and the number of his dialects far greater. In endurance he was the superior of the white man and in intellectual ability Jefferson considered him no whit inferior. It is no wonder that this new character took captive the imagination of the world.

Cooper was not the first to treat Indian character, but he was the first to treat it successfully. When he wrote, there were two schools of opinion about the Indian. The one believed him a demon incarnate, inhuman in all but bodily shape. The only good Indian was a dead Indian. The other considered him an ideal figure, nature's nobleman, the type of what all men once were and might be again. This was the view of Mrs. Behn, of Mrs. Morton, of Voltaire, of Chateaubriand.

Cooper took a middle ground. The Indian was to him first of all a human being of like passions with ourselves. Contrary to the commonly accepted view Cooper did not idealize the Indian. In the works of Parkman and Palfrey it is true that the Indian of Cooper seems to vanish; but in the more recent investigations of Alice Fletcher and Horatio Hale the lost figure reappears and becomes more picturesque and more romantic than Cooper ever dared to portray him. "The instinct of the novelist," as Colonel Higginson has well said, "turned out more authoritative than the premature conclusions of a generation of historians." There is no Indian in Cooper's pages who can compare for a moment in intellectual or moral traits with such historical characters as Pocahontas, Miantonimoh, Massassoit, Hendrick, Occum, or Brant. Occum and Hendrick, it may be added, were both Mohicans and were contemporary with Chingachgook and Uncas.

But whether idealized or not, the Indian of Cooper has, in every part of Europe, made our early history synonymous with romance. He has supplied a means of contrast for our highly institutionalized life. He has furnished the potential material for a national drama and a national opera. He has proved not only the anvil on which we wrought out our national genesis but the background against which Europe contemplates with undiminished interest the early centuries of our national existence.

But if Cooper had never been born, American literature would still have interest for foreigners. Let me remind you that until recently the only recognized types of literature were epic poetry, lyric poetry, dramatic poetry, the essay, the history, the novel, the biography, and the oration. To these must now be added the short story, and in the short story American writers have scored their most distinctive triumph. The short story is not the child of the novel; it is not a story that is merely short. It is a story that could not be longer or shorter—could not be other than it is—without sacrificing its individuality. Professor Brander Matthews suggests that the American short story should be written with a hyphen (short-story) to indicate its distinctiveness as a literary type. Schönbach says that the short story differs from the novel about as much as an example in multiplication differs from the slower process of addition.

The older masters of the American short story were Irving, Poe, Hawthorne, and Bret Harte. These are all widely known in foreign lands, though Poe takes easy precedence among them. Indeed he is justly considered the father of the American short story as a distinctive art creation. His contribution to the short story did not lie in subject matter but in form. His criterion was "totality of effect." The word that best characterizes Poe's constructive art is the word convergence. There are no parallel lines in his best work. With the opening sentence of his stories the lines begin to converge toward a predetermined effect. "If the author's very initial sentence," says Poe, "tend not to the outbringing of this effect, then he has failed in his first step. In the whole composition there should be no word written, of which the tendency, direct or indirect, is not to the one preëstablished design."

Poe's short stories fall into two structural types. In the first, there is an unbroken cumulative movement from the first paragraph to the last; in the second, the mystery deepens in the first half and is completely solved in the second half. The first type may be represented by a capital letter A: the lines of interest converge and culminate at the apex. The second type may be represented by a capital B: the story, in other words, is divided into two equal and corresponding sections or semicircles. To the first class belongs *The Fall of the House of Usher*; to the second class belongs the detective story, of which Poe is justly considered the founder.

The American short story appeals to foreigners because they see certain typical American qualities in its directness of narrative, in its economy of details, in the business-like efficiency with which it goes about its work. There is no formal introduction: it just begins. It does not languish to a conclusion: it simply stops. Its brevity, too, is characteristically American. It consumes in the reading about the same length of time that is spent on a game of football or baseball.

But a more notable service rendered by the American short story, especially since 1870, is that, more than any other form of literature, it has concerned itself with local color, local characters, local history and traditions. We have learned to know the different sections of our own wide country chiefly through the contributions of our short story writers. New England life is reproduced in the works of Sarah Orne Jewett and Mary E. Wilkins; the Middle West lives in the works of Hamlin Garland, Owen Wister, and Mark Twain; the Far West has its historian in Bret Harte; and the South finds its interpreters in George W. Cable, Miss Grace King, Joel Chandler Harris,

James Lane Allen, and Thomas Nelson Page. Other nations have popularized their history through historical novels; since 1870 American writers have popularized their history through short stories. Europe knows us better, therefore, or at least has the opportunity of knowing us better, through our short stories than through our poetry or our novels or our formal histories. It should be said that the excessive use of dialect in American short stories since 1870 has prevented our later writers from being read as widely as they would otherwise have been. In spite of the growing European interest in the negro, for example, no one has attempted a translation of the Uncle Remus Stories.

I need hardly say that another cause of foreign interest in American literature is the prevalence in it of American humor. Whether we like it or not, we are considered funny folks. From Benjamin Franklin to Mark Twain Americans have been the chief purveyors of wholesome merriment. We have not only fired the laugh heard round the world, but we have done more than any other nation to democratize laughter itself. Pretension, hypocrisy, conventionality, pomposity—these are the targets. "At bottom," says Dr. Van Dyke, "American humor is based upon the democratic assumption that the artificial distinctions and conventional phrases of life are in themselves amusing."

When Gladstone was asked what he considered the leading characteristic of American humor he promptly replied "Exaggeration," and illustrated his point by the story of an American merchant who, when the price of ink rose, claimed to have saved a hundred thousand dollars a year by not dotting *i's*. Whether we commend or not the aptness of this illustration, there is no doubt that from the appearance of Irving's *Knickerbocker History of New York* (1809) to the present time exaggeration has been a constituent of American humor, and the suggestion has been made that it is a trait inherited from our Elizabethan ancestors. "Mark Twain," says Professor Brander Matthews, "is the foremost of American humorists because he thus relates us to our [Elizabethan] origins." On the contrary, Mark Twain seems to me the foremost of our humorists not because he suggests the past but solely because he expresses the present. The explanation of exaggeration in American humor is to be sought primarily in the bigness of things that confront the American on all sides. The length of American rivers, the height of American mountains, the distance from North to South and from East to West, the phenomenal growth of American population, the gigantic combinations of American capital, the varied products of American soil,—these things soon begot a sort of interstate and then international rivalry that found ready expression in humorous overstatement.

The foreign view of the magnitude of things American was well expressed by a Frenchman in a footnote to a translation of Cooper's novels. Cooper, you remember, speaks of trees usually by their first names. He does not say a hickory tree or an oak tree or a poplar tree, but a hickory, an oak, a poplar. In one passage he says that Deerslayer dismounted and hitched his horse to the limb of a locust. The Frenchman's dictionary knew no locust but the insect, and so he translated it insect (*sauterelle*), but added the following illuminating note: "In America these insects grow to such a size that horses are often hitched to their dead limbs."

The foreigner's appreciation of the skillful use to which exaggeration is put in American humor may be measured in part by the esteem in which Mark Twain's works are held both in England and on the continent. "Since the death of Charles Dickens," said the *Evening Standard* of London, "no writer of English has been so generally read." "He was more esteemed in Germany," said the *Berliner Zeitung am Mittag*, "than all the French and English humorists put together."

The last characteristic of American literature that I shall mention deserves far more time than can be given it here. It is a characteristic that has been most clearly stated by German critics. In his *History of American Literature* Eduard Engel says: "So far from being contaminated by the American's alleged love of gain getting, so far from being affected by what is proverbially known as Yankeeism, American literature shows decidedly less of these very traits than do the literatures of most other nations. In fact, the fundamental characteristic of American literature is its idealism. All great writers in America—all writers considered great—have been without exception idealists, yes idealists raised to the *n*th power; and it is no accident that from an American poet, from Longfellow, the world has received that exquisite poem whose refrain, 'Excelsior,' has become the watchword of idealists in all lands."

This is high praise to pay American literature but it is abundantly merited. Engel might have mentioned, in addition to Longfellow's familiar poem, Emerson's *Forerunners*, Hawthorne's *Great Stone Face*, Poe's *Eldorado*, Lowell's *L'Envoi to the Muse*, Holmes's *Chambered Nautilus*, Whittier's *Vanishers*, or Lanier's *Song of the Chattahoochee*. They are one and all instinct with an idealism as pure and as high as any literature can show. Indeed *The Great Stone Face* seems to me the highest reach of idealism to which an American short story has ever attained. It sets a standard by which any nation may measure its progress in moral and intellectual worth.

But let me remind you that many of our critics concede idealism to American literature but deny it to American life. This indeed is one of the battlegrounds of conflicting opinion. To my mind the man who sees in the typical American only or chiefly the greedy money-getter or the rabid office-seeker is suffering sorely from spiritual myopia. There are, it must be remembered, two kinds of idealism: the idealism that dreams and the idealism that does. In the former the vision is an end in itself, in the latter it is only a means to an end. The former we may call subjective idealism, the latter constructive idealism. This kind of idealism, the constructive type, has characterized the American people from the beginning. It explains why in the Hall of Fame men of action take precedence over men of abstract thought. It explains the difference in attitude on the part of Americans toward millionaires who inherit or hoard their wealth and those who expend it constructively: we have learned that *richesse oblige.* It explains why Emerson and Jefferson are quoted more often by men of all shades of opinion than any other two writers in our literature. It explains why Poe is coming into his own: we are beginning to recognize that he was essentially American because he was as truly a constructive force in American literature as was Edwards in theology or Jefferson in politics. It explains our loyalty to the stars and bars as well

AMERICANISM OF AMERICAN LITERATURE 33

as to the stars and stripes. It explains the sweep of our civilization westward to the Pacific and across the Pacific to the Philippine Islands. It explains our capacity for expecting great things.

It explains our dissatisfaction with the present condition of our schools and colleges, of our churches and charitable organizations, of our city governments, our state governments, and our national government. This dissatisfaction is not weak or querulous. It is born of an ingrained idealism. It is constructive in its ends and beneficent in its purposes. It is *The Song of the Chattahoochee* set to march time.

The American Indian, the American short story, American humor, and American idealism—these are the elements in our literature that have made the deepest impression upon the European mind. Why? There seems to me only one answer: these are the elements in which the European, consciously or unconsciously, sees or feels something distinctively and essentially American. Other national literatures concern themselves with Indians (or other savage people), with the short story, with humor, with idealism. Indeed I know of no European nation whose literature cannot show notable achievements in all of these reaches of literary effort. But there is something about the American achievement in these things that stamps itself as nationally characteristic. What is it? It is, I believe, the action and interaction of two mighty forces,

forces which have long been recognized in our political life, our religious life, our economic life, and our educational life, but which have not been recognized in our literature. These forces are individualism and collectivism, or, as I prefer to call them, individualism and institutionalism. "Individualism," as defined by ex-President Eliot,[1] "is that tendency in human society to emphasize the rights of each person and to place a high value on initiative." Collectivism is the tendency to distrust individual initiative and to hold "that the interest of the many should override the interest of the individual, and, whenever the two interests conflict, should control social action, and yet does not propose to extinguish the individual but only to restrict him for the common good, including his own." Since 1870 collectivism, as a social force, Dr. Eliot finds, has made steady gains in our industries, education, and government. Evidently Dr. Eliot's definitions avail little in literature where it is not a question of rights, social or otherwise, but a question of how life is looked at and how character is portrayed.

Professor Kuno Francke[2] comments on these two forces, as they manifest themselves in German literature, as follows: "It seems to me that all literary devel-

---

[1] In *The Conflict between Individualism and Collectivism in a Democracy*. (1911).

[2] See his *German Literature as Determined by Social Forces* (1901).

opment is determined by the incessant conflict of two elemental human tendencies: the tendency toward personal freedom and the tendency toward collective organization. The former leads to the observation and representation of whatever is striking, genuine, individual; in short to realism. The latter leads to the observation and representation of whatever is beautiful, significant, universal; in short to idealism." Unchecked individualism may lead to a "vulgar naturalism or to a fanatic mysticism." Unchecked collectivism may lead to "an empty conventionalism."

Without attempting to modify, far less to controvert, the point of view which Professor Francke has so searchingly and brilliantly illustrated in his great book, let us phrase the problem, as it relates to American literature, a little differently. Let us call individualism the tendency to regard and to portray human character as a separate unit. Let us call institutionalism (or collectivism) the tendency to regard and to portray human character in unit groups. An individualist, then, portrays character in the manner of a psychologist; an institutionalist, in the manner of a sociologist. The one views life as so many separate peaks; the other, as a serried range.

De Foe was *par excellence* an individualist when he created the character of Robinson Crusoe. Emerson became the philosopher of individualism when he said: "Society everywhere is in conspiracy against the manhood of every one of its members. Society is a joint stock company, in which the members agree, for the better securing of his bread to each shareholder, to surrender the liberty and culture of the eater." Kipling has illustrated excessive institutionalism in the character of Tomlinson, Thackeray in the character of Becky Sharp. Tomlinson was so unindividual that neither Saint Peter nor the devil could find a place for him; Becky Sharp was so much the prey of the social forces about her that Thackeray himself said he was unable to foresee what she would do at any particular moment.

But what about the Indian? Why, the Indian has played an important role in our literature and in our life partly because he has stimulated thought about the limits of individualism and institutionalism. Never till our forefathers landed at Plymouth Rock and Jamestown had the Anglo-Saxon people been brought into contact with a type of character so un-institutionalized as the American Red Man. This is why our statesmen of Revolutionary times make such frequent references to him. He was a new element in their thinking. They could shun him or shoot him, but there he stood, a supreme type of raw individualism, a concrete example of how much and how little there was in the cry "Back to Nature," which meant "Back to native individualism from a too elaborate institutionalism." We find Jefferson[1] saying: "Were it made a question whether no law, as among the savage Americans [Indians], or too much law as among the civilized Europeans, submits man to the greatest evil, one who has seen both conditions of existence would pronounce it to be the last." This was not the usual view, but Jefferson's words are evidence that the Indian was a whetstone on which both individualist and institutionalist sharpened their weapons of defense. He was a perpetual Robinson Crusoe, a symbol of individualism in its manhood and of institutionalism in its childhood. The Europeans, I am inclined to think, greatly overrate the influence of the Indian upon American life, but there can be no question that in viewing American history through the haze of an Indian summer they have detected some elements, democratic as well as romantic, that would otherwise have passed unregarded.

Coming now to the short story, no one can fail to note since 1870 a triumph for institutionalism. Irving as early as 1820 had emphasized the local or institutional note in *Rip Van Winkle* and *The Legend of Sleepy Hollow*, but he passed almost immediately to *Bracebridge Hall* and *The Tales of a Traveller*, which are not American. Irving was American to the core but he did more to make the legends and traditions of foreign lands known in America than to make the

---
[1] *Notes on Virginia* (1782).

legends and traditions of America known in foreign lands. Edgar Allan Poe, the founder of the earlier American short story, was first and last an individualist. His characters have no trace of the soil about them. They are studies in intellectual analysis rather than in American institutions. But Bret Harte and his compeers, who inaugurated the new movement in 1870, studied not only the individual whom they wished to portray but all the environmental and institutional influences that went to make him what he was.

Edward Eggleston gives the creed of the entire school in these words:[1] "If I were a dispassionate critic and were set to judge my own novels as the writings of another, I should say that what distinguished them from other works of fiction is the prominence which they give to social conditions; that the individual characters are here treated to a greater degree than elsewhere as parts of a study of a society—as in some sense the logical results of the environment. Whatever may be the rank assigned to these stories as works of literary art, they will always have a certain value as materials for the student of social history. Not that in writing them any such purpose was consciously present; it is what we do without exactly intending it that is most characteristic." Bret Harte voices the same general opinion. Though Poe and

---

[1] *The Forum*, November, 1890.

Hawthorne, he says,[1] wrote excellent short stories, "their work did not indicate sufficient knowledge of American geography." By American geography Harte means more than mere place; he means the distinctive institutions of American society as conditioned by locality. He has in mind "the instinct of vicinage," as Howells uses the phrase in this sentence:[2] "If the reader will try to think what the state of polite learning would now be among us, if each of our authors had studied to ignore, as they have each studied to recognize, the value of the character and tradition nearest about them, I believe he will agree with me that we owe everything that we now are in literature to their instinct of vicinage." Now the "instinct of vicinage" lies at the basis of representative institutionalism in literature, and this instinct, though not wholly absent from our short stories written before 1870, did not become dominant and characteristic until the decades following.

In American humor the question is, Do we laugh *with* the individual and *at* the group, or *at* the individual and *with* the group? The answer is not far to seek: the American people laugh with the individual, with the man who maintains an indefeasible possession of himself; they laugh at the man whom the con-

---
[1] *The Cornhill Magazine*, July, 1899.
[2] *The North American Review*, March, 1910. He is discussing Mr. Harrben's Georgia fiction.

ventional trappings of institutionalism seem to have de-individualized and thus to have converted into the complacent representative of a group. The butt is usually an office-holder, because in the popular mind the toga of office, whether in church or state, tends to institutionalize. The officer becomes the man on horseback, and in wit-combats popular sympathy is overwhelmingly with the pedestrian. One illustration will suffice. You remember the story that sent John Allen of Mississippi, to Congress. He had been a private in the War, his competitor a high officer. The most fetching appeal that Allen's competitor used to make was his vivid description of the night before Gettysburg. Allen found it hard to offset this appeal which ran about as follows: "Fellow citizens, go with me in imagination to the night preceding the awful carnage of Gettysburg. Can I ever forget it? Never. I lay in my tent thinking of the morrow. Naught was heard but the drip, drip, drip of the pitiless rain, and the tramp, tramp, tramp of the lone sentinel who guarded my tent." "I was that lone sentinel," called out Mr. Allen, and the tables were immediately and effectually turned. That seems to me eminently characteristic of American humor and equally characteristic of the American people. It is not that we sympathize with the underdog—though we do—it is rather our instinctive belief that the unofficered individual is more genuine, more real, more deserving than the man whom fortune has clothed with some form of institutionalism.

Mark Twain seems to me our most representative humorist, because he is invaribly for the individual and against the institution. Read him again and note how consistently the laugh is at the expense of the man who holds an office and who may therefore be considered as not so much an individual as the representative of a group, the exponent of institutionalism. American humor stands squarely by Burns' ringing words:

> "A prince can mak' a belted knight,
> A marquis, duke, an' a' that;
> But an honest man's aboon his might,
> Guid faith he mauna fa' that!
> For a' that, an' a' that,
> Their dignities, an' a' that,
> The pith o' sense, an' pride o' worth,
> Are higher rank than a' that."

In that inspiriting stanza and in the lines,

> "The rank is but the guinea's stamp,
> The man's the gowd for a' that,"

Burns has written the constitution of triumphant democracy and has said incomparably what American humor has been trying to say from Benjamin Franklin to Mr. Dooley.

In conclusion, is our idealism individual or institutional? Does it set a goal for the one or for the many? For both, as it should do. But, as reflected in our literature, there has been an advance from individualism to institutionalism. The masterpieces of American idealism that I mentioned a little while ago cover a period of thirty-six years. Longfellow wrote *Excelsior* in 1841, Lanier wrote *The Song of the Chattahoochee* in 1877. It is not an accident that *Excelsior* expresses a purely individual idealism, the ideal of self-culture, and that Lanier's poem expresses a collective idealism, the ideal of social service. "My purpose," said Longfellow, "was to display the life of a man of genius, resisting all temptations, laying aside all fears, heedless of all warnings, and pressing right on to accomplish his purpose." Note now the passion for community service that Lanier makes the river express:

>"But oh, not the hills of Habersham,
>   And oh, not the valleys of Hall
>Avail: I am fain for to water the plain.
>Downward the voices of Duty call—
>Downward to toil and be mixed with the main;
>The dry fields burn, and the mills are to turn,
>And a myriad flowers mortally yearn,
>And the lordly main from beyond the plain
>   Calls o'er the hills of Habersham,
>   Calls through the valleys of Hall."

AMERICANISM OF AMERICAN LITERATURE 43

The Americanism of American literature consists primarily, then, in the balance and harmony between individualism and institutionalism. American literature shows these two forces to be not antagonistic but complementary. Americanism, ladies and gentlemen, is democracy, and democracy is neither individualism nor institutionalism. It is a blend of the two. Above all, democracy does not mean individualism at war with institutionalism, or institutionalism at war with individualism. It means individualism emancipating and enriching itself through institutionalism; and it means institutionalism steadying and strengthening itself through individualism. The task of the future is not to abolish or to ignore the one or the other, but to make each serve the other and to make both serve the growing demands of a progressive democracy.

LITERATURE IN THE SOUTH[1]

I SHOULD belie the feelings that are uppermost in my heart tonight if I did not at the outset express my sense of appreciation and privilege at being permitted to speak to this audience on so vital a theme as that which your partiality has assigned me. The spectacle of the American people trying to find and to phrase themselves in a national literature, scanning the pages of their history that they may interpret it in terms of distinctive beauty and suggestiveness, has always been to me one of rare and compelling interest. The building of such a literature means the building of a national pantheon where we may conserve the best thought of every passing age for the inspiration of every succeeding age. Thus and thus only shall we transform a union of sovereign States into a union of sovereign ideals and make of democracy no longer an interesting experiment but an assured triumph.

No literature, however, can be truly national unless it is representative, a condition peculiarly difficult in the case of the United States because of the vast extent of territory involved. The most literary nations of the world have been England, France, Germany,

---

[1] An address delivered before the New York Southern Society, April 10, 1908.

Italy, Greece, and Palestine. But the United States is five times as large as these six countries combined. It is no wonder, therefore, that the history of American literature has been the history of vast sections, each endeavoring primarily to interpret its own life. In his lecture on Greek sculpture, Kekule reminds us that the masterpieces of Greek art were produced to meet the demands of a particular time and a definite generation; but these demands were apprehended with such rare insight and fulfilled with such incomparable fidelity that the particular found itself interpreted in terms of the elemental and universal. Shakespeare's lines are as applicable to art as to ethics:

"To thine own self be true
And it must follow, as the night the day,
Thou canst not then be false to any man."

When I speak, therefore, of Southern literature, I do not use the phrase in a narrow or provincial sense. The adjective designates the place of origin but implies no sectionalism of spirit or limitation of appeal. I mean by Southern literature the artesian attempt made on Southern soil to penetrate to the elemental and universal. If you ask me why the phrase Southern literature is more frequently heard than the phrase New England literature, I reply that it is because the New Englanders sank the first wells and with characteristic promptness gave the name American to the first outflowings. Sidney Lanier is as American as Longfellow, and the literature of the South as truly national as that of New England.

Much has been written of late to explain the literary unproductiveness of the Old South, by which I mean the South prior to the year 1870. In oratory and statesmanship the Old South can challenge comparison with any nation and with any age. And the variety of her oratory was equal to its excellence. From the ringing sentences of Patrick Henry, the simple but nation-building utterances of Washington and Jefferson and Madison, the incisive repartee of John Randolph of Roanoke, the interpretative genius of Marshall, the analytic acumen of Calhoun, the impetuous yet graceful periods of Henry Clay, to the spendthrift eloquence of Sergeant Smith Prentiss, there is hardly a note in the whole gamut of civic oratory or constructive statesmanship which the South did not sound and sound with the ease of a master. But in the realm of literature proper,—the realm of the essay, the novel, and the poem—the Old South was as signally deficient as she was illustrious in debate and statecraft.

Before attempting to assign reasons for this literary unproductiveness, I wish to glance briefly at the poetic achievement of the Old South which, though meager, has not been appraised at its true worth. One small volume would hold all of the poems written in the

South before 1870 that seem destined to maintain their place in American literature. Such a volume would contain selections from Edgar Allan Poe, Henry Timrod, Paul Hamilton Hayne, and Father Ryan. The best textbooks of American literature pay just tribute to the works of these four poets, but they fail to record the fact that the Old South was richer in poems than in poets. There are at least seven short poems which, though written by minor poets, have attained such national vogue as to be found in every up-to-date anthology of American poetry or list of most popular American poems. The authors of these seven poems may justly be called "singers of one song," but the lasting acclaim that each song has received reminds us that

"Time, who soonest drops the heaviest things
That weight his pack, will carry diamonds long."

The first of these is *The Star-Spangled Banner* by Francis Scott Key of Maryland. With one exception, that of Hopkinson's *Hail Columbia*, Key's poem is the first permanent contribution made to the patriotic poetry of America and is the only poem of note called forth by the war of 1812. The refrain,

"The land of the free and the home of the brave,"

is at least as widely current a quotation as American literature can show.

In the following year, 1815, appeared *The Captive's Lament* by Richard Henry Wilde, an adopted citizen of Georgia. The poem is better known by its first line, "My life is like the summer rose." The last stanza, though the least familiar, is easily the best:

> "My life is like the prints which feet
>   Have left on Tampa's desert strand;
> Soon as the rising tide shall beat
>   All trace will vanish from the sand.
> Yet, as if grieving to efface
> All vestige of the human race,
> On that lone shore loud moans the sea,
> But none, alas, shall mourn for me!"

The next to the last line has been often cited as a perfect blend of sound and sense, and Byron wrote at once to congratulate Wilde on having written "the finest poem of the century." And yet such was the popular attitude in this country toward the writing of poetry that Wilde was unwilling to admit the authorship of this poem until compelled to deny that it had been written by others.

In 1825 there appeared a thin volume of poems by Edward Coate Pinkney of Maryland. One of these was entitled *A Health,* and it is no disparagement of Ben Johnson's famous lines to say that the English language does not contain a toast the equal of Pinkney's in purity of sentiment or faultlessness of structure:

> "I fill this cup to one made up
>   Of loveliness alone,
> A woman, of her gentle sex
>   The seeming paragon;
> To whom the better elements
>   And kindly stars have given
> A form so fair, that, like the air,
>   'Tis less of earth than heaven.
>
> "Her every tone is music's own,
>   Like those of morning birds.
> And something more than melody
>   Dwells ever in her words;
> The coinage of her heart are they,
>   And from her lips each flows
> As one may see the burdened bee
>   Forth issue from the rose
>
> * * * * * *
>
> "I fill this cup to one made up
>   Of loveliness alone,
> A woman, of her gentle sex
>   The seeming paragon—
> Her health! and would on earth there stood
>   Some more of such a frame,
> That life might be all poetry,
>   And weariness a name."

The next occasional poem to fill a niche in popular appreciation was *Florence Vane*, published in 1847, by Philip Pendleton Cooke, a brother of John Esten Cooke of Virginia. Instead of a selection from this exquisite lyric, which is too close-woven to bear fragmentary quotation, let me substitute an extract from one of Cooke's letters: "What do you think of a friend of mine," he writes, "a most valuable and worthy and hard-riding one, saying gravely to me a short time ago?—'I wouldn't waste time on a d—d thing like poetry. You might make yourself, with all your sense and judgment, a useful man in settling neighborhood disputes and difficulties.' " Beneath the humor of it, which Cooke was broad enough to feel, there is yet the pathos of the chilling environment, the uncongenial public opinion, which in his case and many others made of literature an avocation rather than a vocation.

Near the close of 1847 Theodore O'Hara wrote *The Bivouac of the Dead*. The poem "marched to the front in detachments," quotations from it becoming popular long before the name of the poem or its author was generally known. O'Hara was later a Confederate soldier and the highest tribute to his genius was paid by the men against whom he fought. "A stroll through any of our national cemeteries," says a New York writer, "will suggest the idea that the

War Department has official knowledge of but one elegiac poem."

If *The Bivouac of the Dead* is the best martial elegy in American literature, Randall's *Maryland, My Maryland* is the most stirring martial lyric. Oliver Wendell Holmes voiced the consensus of critical opinion North and South when he pronounced it "the best poem produced on either side during the Civil War." Its occasional intemperance of expression only adds to the faithfulness of its portrayal of contemporary conditions and enables us to measure the distance traversed from that day to this. The appearance of Mr. Randall at the Jamestown Exposition on "Maryland Day" as the guest of honor of the people of Maryland was a beautiful tribute of the industrial New South to the literary Old South, and his death three months ago marked the passing of the last figure that helped to make illustrious the annals of our antebellum literature.

The last poem that I shall mention, *Little Giffen of Tennessee,* by Dr. Francis O. Ticknor of Georgia, appeared in 1867 in the columns of *The Land We Love,* a magazine edited at Charlotte, North Carolina, by General D. H. Hill. It is the true story of a wounded Confederate boy who was nursed back to health by Doctor and Mrs. Ticknor. But in a larger sense it typifies the story of hundreds of young Confederate heroes, mere striplings, in whose boy hands the sword was mightier than the pen. In the simplicity of its pathos, the intensity of its appeal, and the dramatic compression of its thought, *Little Giffen,* though last in time, is first in rank of all the poems yet cited:

"Out of the foremost and focal fire,
Out of the hospital walls as dire,
Smitten of grapeshot and gangrene,
Eighteenth battle and he sixteen—
Specter such as you seldom see,
Little Giffen of Tennessee.

" 'Take him and welcome,' the surgeon said,
'Not the doctor can help the dead.'
So we took him and brought him where
The balm was sweet in our summer air;
And we laid him down on a wholesome bed,
Utter Lazarus, heel to head!

"And we watched the war with abated breath!
Skeleton boy 'gainst skeleton death!
Months of torture, now many such!
Weary weeks of the stick and the crutch,—
And still a glint in the steel-blue eye
Told of a spirit that wouldn't die.

"And didn't! Nay, more, in death's despite
The crippled skeleton learned to write.
'Dear Mother,' at first, of course, and then

'Dear Captain,' inquiring about the men.
Captain's answer: 'Of eighty and five
Giffen and I are left alive.'

" 'Johnston pressed at the front,' they say;
Little Giffen was up and away.
A tear, his first, as he bade good-by,
Dimmed the glint of his steel-blue eye;
'I'll write, if spared.' There was news of the fight
But none of Giffen—he did not write.

"I sometimes fancy that were I king
Of the courtly knights of Arthur's ring,
With the voice of the minstrel in mine ear
And the tender legend that trembles here,—
I'd give the best on his bended knee,
The whitest soul of my chivalry,
For little Giffen of Tennessee."

Such, then, was the contribution to American literature of some of the minor poets of the South, a contribution ignored in current textbooks of American literature because these treat of poets rather than of poems. When we add to these seven poems the more voluminous contributions of Hayne, Timrod, and especially Poe, whose influence on foreign literatures far exceeds that of any other American poet, it must be conceded that the contribution of the Old South to the poetry of the nation has been generally underrated. The question, however, still confronts us, why was not the South before 1870 more distinctively literary?

The problem is a difficult one. The Southern people were of almost unmixed Anglo-Saxon stock. Their social refinement, their responsive temperament, and their quick intelligence were matters of frequent comment by outside visitors. Their intellectual vigor and administrative efficiency were exemplified in the careers of numerous political and military leaders. They lived close to nature and knew her laws. The romantic charm of their colonial and revolutionary history drew from Bryant his *Song of Marion's Men*, from Longfellow his *Evangeline*, and from Thackeray his *Virginians*. Copies of Shakespeare, Milton, Addison, and Scott were found in every cultured home. A New York bookseller wrote that his costliest invoices of European literature went "to the old mansions on the banks of the James and the Savannah and the bluffs of the Mississippi."

Joseph Le Conte, the great geologist, in his recent autobiography relates that he learned from the lips of a South Carolina planter his first lessons in evolution long before Darwin had published his great work. "Nothing could be more remarkable," adds Le Conte, "than the wide reading, the deep reflection, the refined culture, and the originality of thought and observation characteristic of them [the Southern planters];

LITERATURE IN THE SOUTH 55

and yet the idea of publication never entered their heads."

It was not, then, to lack of culture that lack of literature must be accredited. Other reasons must be sought. Mr. Philip Alexander Bruce, the scholarly historian of Virginia, says: "The only plausible reason is that, unlike Old England and New England, the Southern States before the abolition of slavery were entirely lacking in a literary center," there being "no city in the South approaching either London or Boston." Mr. Thomas Nelson Page adduces five reasons:

(1) "The people of the South were an agricultural people, widely diffused, and lacking the stimulus of immediate mental contact.

(2) "The absence of cities, which in the history of literary life have proved literary foci essential for its production, and the want of publishing-houses in the South.

(3) "The exactions of the institution of slavery, and the absorption of the intellectual forces of the people of the South in the solution of the vital problems it engendered.

(4) "The general ambition of the Southern people for political distinction, and the application of their literary powers to polemical controversy.

(5) "The absence of a reading public in the South for American authors, due in part to the conservatism of the Southern people."

It seems to me that the different reasons advanced may all be subsumed under one unitary principle, a principle which finds abundant illustration in the history of England and America. Great literary movements are the expression of national awakenings. They pre-suppose a quickening of the national life and a broadening of the national outlook. They imply the presence of some mighty influence that brings about community of interest and effort together with the emancipation of hope and vision. Such an influence must integrate rather than sectionalize. There must be provided also the material means of embodying and diffusing the new ideals. Literature on a large scale implies authorship as a profession, and authorship as a profession has never flowered among a poor people. These twofold conditions, the twin demands of spirit and body, are more nearly fulfilled by great industrial movements than by any other movements known to history. Literary productiveness, in other words, is vitally related to industrial productiveness, both being correlative manifestations of the creative spirit.

No more striking confirmation of this principle could be adduced than the fact that every great industrial era in English and American history has ac-

LITERATURE IN THE SOUTH 57

companied or immediately preceded a literary era. As this fact has been generally overlooked, let me call briefly to your attention the three great industrial periods of modern times. I shall merely sketch these periods, leaving to you the pleasure of filling in the outlines at your leisure. The facts are undisputed and may be found in any up-to-date history of modern industrialism.

(1) The first industrial revolution came in the reign of Elizabeth (1558-1603). All through the Middle Ages the little country of Flanders, just across the channel from England, had been the manufactory of Europe. England did not manufacture her own wool; she sent it to Flanders, to be received back in fine textile goods. But in the reign of Queen Eliabeth, for reasons which I need not enumerate, Flemish refugees came to England, taught the English peasantry their industrial arts, and, for the first time, England ceased to be dependent on Flanders and became herself a wool manufacturing country. This economic change is of vast significance, and the parallel between the industrial conditions of Eliabeth's reign and the industrial conditions in the South since 1870 is full of interest and suggestiveness. In this parallel cotton replaces wool, for cotton did not then figure in English history as an industrial factor.

The manufacturing population was not confined to the English towns, but spread all over the country.

Even North England, which had lagged far behind South England (here we must reverse our parallel), now showed signs of intense industrial activity and entered into healthy competition with the more southern sections. Of course it was all domestic manufacture; it was handiwork. But England increased rapidly in wealth, in commercial power, in all that constitutes material prosperity.

The keels of Elizabeth's bold freebooters, Raleigh, Drake, Frobisher, and Hawkins, vexed all seas and brought treasure from all shores. Sir Thomas Gresham founded the first Royal Exchange. England felt as never before the thrill of a new industrial life and the thrill of a rounded nationalism born of industrial freedom. I have often thought that when Shakespeare speaks so proudly of,

"This happy breed of men, this little world,
This precious stone set in the silver sea,
This blessed plot, this earth, this realm, this England,"

there passed before his eye not only a vision of armed and warlike England girt by fearless defenders, but a vision of happy English homes filled with the peace and contentment that spring from self-supporting toil.

Elizabeth's reign was, then, peculiarly an industrial epoch. I need not tell you that her reign was and is the glory of English letters. It is needless to rehearse those illustrious names that will perish only with the

LITERATURE IN THE SOUTH 59

language that you and I speak. My purpose is merely to show that in this wonderful period literature found a friend in industrialism. Both were agencies of national expression. Industrialism spoke in works, literature in words. And if industrialism deepened the sense of national greatness, literature gave voice to the new consciousness.

(2) Let us pass now to another industrial revolution nearer our own time. In 1775, a memorable date in our history, James Watt began the manufacture of steam-engines. The change from the domestic system of industrialism to the modern method of production by machinery and steam-power was sudden and violent. Before the year 1800 all the great inventions of Watt, Arkwright, Boulton, and Hargreaves had been completed and the modern factory system inaugurated. The writers on industrial history tell us that "England increased her wealth tenfold and gained a hundred years' start in front of the nations of Europe." In fifteen years (1788-1803) the cotton trade trebled itself.

Of course vigorous protests were made against this spirit of rampant industrialism. Thomas DeQuincey, then only fifteen years of age, complained in 1800 that he could not stir out of doors without being "nosed by a factory, a cotton bag, a cotton dealer, or something else allied to that detestable commerce." The

Jeremiahs and Cassandras believed that everything was going to the "demnition bow-wows."

But what was literature doing? She was witnessing a renaissance second only to that of "the spacious times of great Elizabeth." This was her romantic period, her liberal era, the age that nourished Keats, Shelley, Byron, Scott, Coleridge, Wordsworth, Burns, and Burke. In a love of nature that made all seasons seem as spring, in devotion to democratic ideals, in variety and range and intensity of feeling, this period takes precedence of Elizabeth's reign. The literary outburst can best be described in Coleridge's lines:

"And now 'twas like all instruments,
   Now like a lonely flute;
And now it was an angel's song
   That makes the heavens be mute."

It was of this age that Wordsworth said:

"Joy was it in that dawn to be alive,
But to be young was very heaven."

(3) There has been but one other great industrial era marked by wide-reaching discovery and fruitful invention. It falls within the fifteen years from 1830 to 1845. Those years are the storage battery of both the industrial and the literary forces that have shaped the Victorian era. In those years railroads first began to intersect the land, telegraph lines were first

LITERATURE IN THE SOUTH 61

stretched, and the ocean was crossed for the first time by steam-propelled vessels. All of these mechanical triumphs tended to annihilate time and space. The products of manufacturing could now be sent to the most distant quarters. Nations came closer together. The two hemispheres became and have continued one vast arena of industrial interchange. Even Tennyson catches the industrial inspiration, and in 1842 celebrates in the same breath the glories of invention and the triumphs of commerce:

"For I dipt into the future, far as human eye could see,
Saw the vision of the world, and all the wonder that
    would be;
"Saw the heavens fill with commerce, argosies of
    magic sails
Pilots of the purple twilight, dropping down with
    costly bales."

But let us look at the purely literary record of these years. The English writers who dominated the literary life of the Victorian era, and who bid fair to dominate many decades of our present century, are Tennyson, Browning, and Mrs. Browning in poetry; Dickens, Thackeray, and George Eliot in fiction; Ruskin and Carlyle in miscellaneous literature. Every one of these writers rose to prominence between 1830 and 1845. Before 1830 they were unknown; by 1845, not to know them was to confess inexcusable ignorance.

But our own country furnishes as striking illustrations. Of the three industrial movements enumerated, the first could, of course, have no effect upon American life, the initial settlements at Jamestown and Plymouth Rock being themselves a part of the mighty influence that made Shakespeare and the Elizabethan age possible. The second industrial revolution, that beginning in 1775, found also no foothold upon American soil. The thirteen colonies were struggling for their very existence as an independent people. There was neither time nor opportunity for great industrial changes or for community of literary effort. Leadership was necessarily either political or military.

By 1830, however, when the third industrial revolution began, there was one section of our country peculiarly adapted to prove hospitable to it. The New England States, by their small holdings instead of large plantations, by their harbor facilities and rapid rivers, by their township groupings and the resultant ascendancy of the meeting house, by the very texture of their institutional life, were admirably fitted to assimilate the new influences and to assume at once the industrial leadership. This they did, and the change in their literary life was as instantly manifest. Before 1830 New England had no distinctive literature, but by 1840 she was represented by Longfellow, Lowell, Whittier, Hawthorne, Emerson, and Holmes, the six names that have given the New England States their incontestable supremacy in American literature.

Why did not the South respond to this literary and industrial movement? Why did she wait until 1870? Because in 1830 her energies began to be more and more absorbed in defense of her constitutional views and of her cherished institutions. The year 1830 that ushered in the era of opportunity to others, saw the memorable debate between Robert Y. Hayne, of South Carolina, and Daniel Webster—the most significant contest that the senate of the United States has ever witnessed. It was the opening cannon of a struggle that was to end only on the field of Appomattox. Sectional lines began to be drawn closer and closer. The South was thrown more and more on the defensive. She was shut in more and more from outside influences. Her industrial system, based on slave labor, stood as a barrier to the new industrial movement; and the enforced defense of this system, together with the political problems and prejudices that it engendered, threw literature into the background and brought oratory and statesmanship to the front.

But a change came at last and in the storm and night of war the old order passed, yielding place to new. The ultimate literary significance of the Civil War you and I may not live to see, but if history proves anything it proves that literature loves a lost cause, provided honor be not lost. Hector, the leader of the defeated Trojans, Hector the warrior, slain in defense of his own fireside, is the most princely figure that the Greek Homer has portrayed. The Roman Virgil is proud to trace the lineage of his people not back to the victorious Greeks, but on to the defeated Trojans. England's greatest poet laureate finds his amplest inspiration not in the victories of his Saxon ancestors over King Arthur, but in King Arthur himself and his peerless Knights of the Round Table, vanquished though they were in battle. And so it has always been; the brave but unfortunate reap always the richest measure of literary immortality.

Do you remember that tender scene in King Lear, where Cordelia stands in the presence of her father, despised, disinherited, forsaken? As her cowardly suitor slinks from the room because Cordelia's inheritance has been lost, the King of France steps forward and on bended knee says:

"Fairest Cordelia, that art most rich, being poor;
Most choice, forsaken; and most loved, despised;
Thee and thy virtues here I seize upon;
Be it lawful, I take up what's cast away."

And so when brave men have fought for the right, as God gave them to see the right, but fought in vain; when the bugles call no more; when the banners are tattered and trailing; when the shouts of victory are forever hushed, and the *miserere* of defeat is chanted over the graves of a buried army; when all, all, is lost save honor, it is then that the muses of poetry and song stoop from their celestial heights and lift the dear old lost cause up, up, into the unchanging realm of literature.

We are still too near to that great struggle to trace the exact orbit of its influence upon the poetry of the future. It will doubtless find expression in some stately epic or in some cluster of great dramas. There will be no bitterness in the story, no note of grievance, no weak or passionate regret. There will be only the common love of the heroic and the beautiful. A united nation will find in it the treasury of a sacred past, the pledge and promise of an enduring future.

The immediate effect of the Civil War, however, was industrial and economic. The South had not before undergone any essential change in her industrial system, but no part of the country has ever undergone so sudden and so radical an upheaval. Influences from without and impulses from within, both of which, forty years before, had beat unavailingly against the barriers of an antiquated system, now passed freely through open doors. Literature was not slow to heed the challenge of the time. With new economic ideas, with an ever-increasing development of her natural resources, with a subdivision of her ancestral lands, with a more flexible industrial system, with a more rational attitude toward labor, and more diffused facilities for knowledge, there came to the South a literary inspiration impossible before. And the year 1870, which statisticians take as the birth-year of the new industrial movement in the South, is also the birth-year of the new literary movement. The open door of 1870 has more than made amends for the closed door of 1830. The words which Sidney Lanier wrote to his wife in 1870 may be taken in a larger sense than he meant them: "Day by day . . . a thousand vital elements rill through my soul. Day by day the secret deep forces gather, which will presently display themselves in bending leaf and waxy petal and in useful fruit and grain."

Hardly were those words written before Irwin Russell, of Mississippi, opened a new province to American literature by his skillful delineations of negro character. In 1872 Maurice Thompson is hailed by Longfellow as "a new and original singer, fresh, joyous, and true." In 1875 Sidney Lanier attains national fame, and the six years of life that remained to him were to be filled with bursts of imperishable song. In 1876 Joel Chandler Harris annexed the province that Irwin Russell had discovered, and "Uncle Remus" quietly assumed a place in the literature of humor and folklore never filled till then. In

1878 Miss Murfree, better known as Charles Egbert Craddock, began her inimitable sketches of the illiterate mountaineers of East Tennessee. The decade closed with the appearance in literature of George W. Cable, whose *Grandissimes*, however questionable as history, is unquestionable as art.

The next decade, that from 1880 to 1890, witnessed the advent of Mr. Thomas Nelson Page, Mr. James Lane Allen, and Mr. Madison Cawein. Mr. Page in his *Marse Chan* and *Meh Lady* not only presented the relation of master and slave in a new light, but furnished at the same time the long-looked-for exposure of the latent injustice and one-sidedness of *Uncle Tom's Cabin*. The historical value to the South, therefore, of stories like these, to say nothing of their literary charm, cannot be easily overrated. Mr. Allen in his *Sketches of the Blue Grass Region of Kentucky* brought another state into the literary union and spread the charm of a storied past over a region that had long ago led Henry Ward Beecher to say: "Henceforth, to me, the twenty-third psalm shall read, 'He maketh me to lie down in blue grass pastures.'" Mr. Cawein in his *Blooms of the Berry* struck clearly, if tentatively, the first note of a song that was later to approve him the great nature poet of his age. "No other poet," Mr. Howells has just said, "not even of the great Elizabethan range, can outword this poet when it comes to choosing some epithet fresh from the earth or air, and with the morning sun or light upon it, for an emotion or experience in which the race renews its youth from generation to generation." It is from Louisville, Kentucky, writes Mr. Edmund Gosse, that "the only hermit-thrush now seems to sing." But I need not call the roll further. It is enough to say that in 1888, just eighteen years after the beginning of the new movement, ex-Judge Albion W. Tourgee, whom no one could charge with undue Southern sympathies, declared (in *The Forum* of December) that a foreigner studying the contemporary literature of the United States "without knowledge of our history, and judging our civilization by our fiction, would undoubtedly conclude that the South was the seat of intellectual empire in America." What a literary revolution do those words indicate!

This is neither the time nor the place to attempt an appraisal of the new school of Southern writers. But they are rendering one service so signal in importance that it cannot be overlooked in even the most cursory survey of their work. It is often said that the South has produced no historian and that her history remains, therefore, unknown. The real historians of the South are the writers whom I have mentioned. Enshrine history in literature and you give it both currency and permanency. The world knows Scottish history not from Burton's learned volumes but from the glowing pages of Walter Scott and Robert Burns.

> "And what for this frail world, were all
>   That mortals do or suffer,
> Did no responsive harp, no pen,
>   Memorial tribute offer?"

The formal historian may galvanize the past, but the poet and story-teller vitalize it.

When Rufus Choate, in 1833, made his impassioned plea for the perpetuation of New England history by a series of poems and romances, the outlook was far from encouraging. New England had then no distinctive literature, nor had a single poet or prose-writer touched with the wand of his genius any event or locality in New England history. But in less than ten years from the time of Mr. Choate's address Emerson had written his great *Concord Hymn,* and Hawthorne his *Twice-Told Tales.* The movement was now on, and in rapid succession *Mosses from an Old Manse, The Scarlet Letter, The House of the Seven Gables, The Courtship of Miles Standish,* and *Paul Revere's Ride* completed a cycle that has done more to popularize the history of Massachusetts than all the historians from William Bradford to John Fiske.

It is an interesting fact in the history of American literature that Longfellow himself began his poetical career by finding his inspiration and his themes in the history and legends of foreign lands. But the criticism of Margaret Fuller led him to see that his own country had poetical material as well as Spain and Germany. It was then that Longfellow gave to the world his trilogy of poems dealing with American life. And *Evangeline, Hiawatha,* and *The Courtship of Miles Standish* remain today as Longfellow's surest guarantee of immortality. Southern writers do not merit the rebuke of Margaret Fuller, for they are finding their themes and their inspiration in the life that is near and dear to them. They are not rising into solitary and selfish renown; they are lifting the South with them. They are writing Southern history because they are interpreting Southern life.

HISTORICAL TENDENCIES IN RECENT SOUTHERN LITERATURE [1]

I

THE YEAR 1870 marks an epoch in the history of the South. It witnessed not only the death of Robert E. Lee but the passing also of John Pendleton Kennedy, George Denison Prentice, Augustus Baldwin Longstreet, and William Gilmore Simms. In literature it was not only the end of the old but the beginning of the new, for in 1870 the new movement in Southern literature may be said to have been inaugurated in the work of Irwin Russell. I have attempted elsewhere to trace briefly the chronological outlines of this literature from 1870 to the present time. In this paper, therefore, I shall discuss not the history *of* this literature but rather the history *in* this literature.

Much has been spoken and written of late about the need in our schools of better histories of the South. I for one care little where a history hails from, provided it be true in matter, interesting in treatment, and adapted to the needs of the class. The important thing is not authorship but craftsmanship. It must not be overlooked, however, that formal text-books of history, however well written, can never carry as

---
[1] Reprinted from *The Southern Review*, January, 1920.

far as history translated into literature. Wellington said that all the English history he knew he learned from Shakespeare. Lowell declared Hawthorne's *House of the Seven Gables* "the most valuable contribution to New England history that has yet been made."

It is not the painstaking investigator alone who can contribute to history. The finer work of giving color, coherence, symmetry, and vitality must come from the literary artist. We need both kinds of workmen; but the latter alone can confer universality upon the work of the former. Enshrine history in literature and you give it both currency and permanency.

Now when we compare Southern literature of antebellum days with that produced since 1870 we note at once certain obvious differences of style and structure. In the older literature the sentences are longer, the paragraphs less coherent, adjectives more abundant, descriptions more elaborate, plots more intricate and fanciful. In the newer literature the pen is held more firmly; there are fewer episodes; incidents are chosen to illustrate character rather than to enhance the plot; the language is more temperate; the pathos and humor more subtle; some fixed goal is kept in view and the action of the story converges steadily toward this end.

RECENT SOUTHERN LITERATURE 73

II

But apart from these stylistic and structural differences there are differences that appeal to the student of history equally as much as to the student of literature. Since 1870 Southern writers have begun to find their topics and their inspiration in the life that is round about them. They are resorting not so much to books as to memory, observation, and experience. They are not rising into solitary and selfish renown; they are lifting the South with them. They are writing Southern history because they are describing Southern life. The writings of Irwin Russell, Sidney Lanier, Joel Chandler Harris, Armistead Gordon, Thomas Nelson Page, George W. Cable, Charles Egbert Craddock, John Fox, Jr., James Lane Allen, Grace King, Ruth McEnery Stuart, Princess Troubetzkoy, Harry Stillwell Edwards, Mary Johnston, Ellen Glasgow, John Charles McNeil, Sarah Barnwell Elliott, Robert Burns Wilson, Kate Chopin, Francis Hopkinson Smith, Olive Tilford Dargan, Alice Hegan Rice, Hallie Erminie Rives-Wheeler, James Branch Cabell, Mrs. Lucian Cocke, Margaret Busbee Shipp, O. Henry, Archibald Henderson, Will Harben, Irvin Cobb, James Hay, Jr., Octavius Roy Cohen, and Corra May Harris are spreading a knowledge of Southern life and Southern ideals where such knowledge has never penetrated before. Though we call this literature Southern, it is neither sectional in its appeal nor provincial in its outlook. It is American to the core, American *via* its Southernism, and Southern *via* its Americanism.

It has long seemed to me that much of the immediate influence of *Uncle Tom's Cabin* both in this country and in England was due to the fact that the South could not show in all of its ante-bellum literature a single novel treating the same themes treated by Mrs. Stowe, but treating them from a different point of view. It was the first attempt to portray in vivid colors the social and institutional conditions of the South. None of our writers had utilized the material that lay ready to their hands. There was no story written in the spirit of *Marse Chan* or *Uncle Remus* which the South could hold up and say,

"Look here, upon this picture, and on this."

The reception accorded Mrs. Stowe's book in the South teaches a valuable lesson, and a lesson which Southern writers have for fifty years profited by. *Uncle Tom's Cabin* was met by bitter criticism, by argument, by denunciation, by denial, or by contemptuous silence. But the appeal made by a literary masterpiece, however deficient or faulty in its premises, is not thus to be negatived. The true answer to *Uncle Tom's Cabin* and the most adequate answer that could be given is to be found in the historical note that characterizes the work of Irwin Russell and those who have succeeded him.

Irwin Russell was the first of the new school to fall on sleep; but his influence, perpetuated more notably through Joel Chandler Harris and Thomas Nelson Page, has been distinctive and crescent. His priority in the fictional use of the negro dialect has been frequently emphasized, but I wish to emphasize his priority in utilizing for literary purposes the social and institutional conditions in which he himself had lived. Skill in the use of a dialect is a purely literary excellence, but when a writer portrays and thus perpetuates the peculiar life of a people numbering four million, he is to that extent an historian; and Irwin Russell's example in this respect meant a complete change of front in Southern literature. He did not go to Italy for his inspiration as Richard Henry Wilde had done. You find no *Rodolph*, or *Hymns to the Gods*, or *Voyage to the Moon* among his writings; but you find that deeper poetic vision that saw pathos and humor and beauty in the humble life that others had condemned.

The appearance of *Christmas-Night in the Quarters* meant that Southern literature was now to become a true reproduction of Southern conditions. Our writers were henceforth to busy themselves with the interpretation of life at close range. They were to produce a kaleidoscopic body of fiction, each bit of which, sparkling with its own characteristic and independent color, should yet contribute its part to the harmony and symmetry of the national whole.

I would not for a moment compare the genius of Irwin Russell with that of Chaucer or of Burns; and yet when Chaucer, in the latter part of his life, turned from French and Italian sources to find an ampler inspiration in his own England, the England that he knew and loved, he was but illustrating the change that Irwin Russell was to inaugurate in Southern literature; and when Robert Burns broke through the classical trammels of the eighteenth century and lifted the poor Scotch cotter into the circle of the immortals, he was but anticipating the Mississippian in proving that poetry, like charity, begins at home. To the student of literature, there is a wide difference between the *Prologue to the Canterbury Tales,* *The Cotter's Saturday Night,* and the *Christmas-Night in the Quarters;* but to the student of history the poems stand upon the same plane because each is a transcript of contemporary life.

Irwin Russell represents, therefore, a transition of vital significance in our literature, a transition that had been partly foretold in the work of Judge Longstreet and Col. Richard Malcolm Johnston. There is as much local coloring in the *Georgia Scenes* and the *Dukesborough Tales* as in the work of Irwin Russell; but I do not find the same deft workmanship; I miss in the older works the sympathy, the pathos, and the self-restraint that enable Irwin Russell to be local in his themes without being provincial in his manner.

I do not say that the poet or the novelist must never revert to past history or to historical documents for his topics. His own genius and taste must be his surest guide both as to topic and to treatment; but I do say that a nation is unfortunate if the builders of its literature invaribly draw their material from foreign sources or from the history that was enacted before they were born.

The historical element, therefore, of which I am speaking is not synonymous with the historical novel. The critics apply the term historical to those novels that attempt to reproduce the past. These novels are retrospective and essentially romantic. In the work of Walter Scott this form of literature attained its florescence. But I contend that while the historical novel may have a genuinely human interest, its value as history is almost inappreciable as compared with the historical value of the literature that portrays contemporary life. We do not study ancient history in Chaucer's *Legend of Good Women,* but there would be a deplorable gap in our knowledge of fourteenth century England if the *Prologue to the Canterbury Tales* had never been written.

A hundred years from now Dickens's *Tale of Two Cities* will not have the historical significance that *David Copperfield* will have; because the *Tale of Two Cities* is based on records that are accessible to all students of the French Revolution. It is not an interpretation of life at first hand: it is an interpretation only of books. Then, too, historical investigation is even today far more accurate and scientific than when Dickens wrote. But *David Copperfield*, which the critics have never called an historical novel, has an historical element that time cannot take away, for it is the record of what an accurate observer saw and felt and heard in the first half of the nineteenth century. The historical novel, therefore, in the current acceptation of the term, contributes nothing to the sources of historical study. Its distinctive value is that it popularizes history and thus helps to prepare an audience for the scientific historian.

Now the South has produced her full share of historical novels, if we use the term in its traditional sense. From Kennedy's *Horse Shoe Robinson* in 1835 to Mary Johnston's *Cease Firing* in 1912, Southern writers have shown themselves by no means insensible to the literary possibilities latent in our colonial and revolutionary and civil war history. But it was not until 1870 that the South may be said to have had a school of writers who, while not neglecting the historical novel proper, began to find the scenery and materials of their stories chiefly in local conditions and in passing or remembered events. Much, it is true, has been lost to our literature, but much has been saved.

It has often been said that the new movement in Southern literature was due to the influence of Bret Harte's works, but such a statement hardly deserves refutation. The cause lies far deeper than this. The events of 1861-1865 not only broke the continuity of Southern history but changed forever the social and economic status of the Southern states. The past began to loom up strange and remote, but "dear as remembered kisses after death." Men seemed to have lived a quarter of a century in four years. They moved as in a world not realized. Now it is just at such periods that literature finds its opportunity, for at such periods a people's historic consciousness is either deepened or destroyed, and this national consciousness finds expression in historical literature.

III

The South, then, for the last fifty years has been writing her history in her literature. The measure of her success in this high enterprise may be gauged in part from a sheaf of outside opinions. In 1880, Horace E. Scudder said, in the *Atlantic Monthly:*

"The South is still a foreign land to the North." Eight years later, Albion W. Tourgee wrote, in *The Forum:* "It cannot be denied that American fiction of today, whatever may be its origin, is predominantly Southern in type and character. . . . A foreigner studying our current literature, without knowledge of our history, and judging our civilization by our fiction, would undoubtedly conclude that the South was the seat of intellectual empire in America."

In 1915 Fred Lewis Pattee reviewed the movement in these words: "The cause of the Southern tone which American literature took on during the eighties lies in the single fact that the South had the literary material. The California gold, rich as it was when first discovered by the East, was quickly exhausted. There were no deep mines; it was surface gold, pockets, and startling nuggets. Suddenly it was discovered that the South was a field infinitely richer, and the tide turned. Nowhere else were to be found such a variety of picturesque types of humanity: negroes, crackers, creoles, mountaineers, moonshiners, and all those incongruous elements that had resulted from the great social upheaval of 1861-1865. Behind it in an increasingly romantic perspective lay the old regime destroyed by the war; nearer was the war itself, most heroic of struggles; and still nearer was the tragedy of reconstruction with its carpetbagger, its freed slaves, and its Ku-Klux terror. Never before in America, even in California, had there been such richness of literary material. That a group of Southern-born writers should have arisen to deal with it was inevitable. Who else *could* have dealt with it, especially in the new era that demanded reality and absolute genuineness?"

The movement has not slackened but, if it is to carry on, there is one insistent and essential need that cannot be overlooked. There must be developed in the South a finer and more standardized critical sense. Criticism, ceasing to be provincial, must become balanced, just, liberal, and unafraid. Southern writers ask no critical favors and should receive none. They ask and they need a standard of criticism as varied as literature itself is varied but centralized by good taste, reasoned sympathy, and institutional understanding. And the organ of this criticism, if it is to function properly, should be established in the South. It should know what has been done but set its face all the more resolutely toward the wider domain of what is still to be done. Its arena should be not only regional but national and international. To be less than this is in this day to be parochial. Its aim should be neither to slash nor to slush but to understand, then to appraise, then to build and to help build.

Above all, from its pages should be sounded resonantly and consistently the historical note of which I have spoken. If it can bring history and literature into still closer accord, if it can interpret the historian to the litterateur and the litterateur to the historian, it will not only release the springs of a larger power in both but will inaugurate a movement more fruitful and beneficent than that sketched in these pages.

SOUTHERN ORATORY BEFORE THE WAR

THE INFLUENCE of great orators, like the influence of great musicians, has never, I think, received adequate recognition at the hands of historians. The true king of a people is frequently not the monarch on the throne, but he whose speech can convert vast multitudes into one man, giving them one heart, one pulse, one voice. His trumphs are instantaneous: they follow his efforts as the thunder peal follows the lightning's flash. He does not have to wait for coming generations to yield him the merited meed of praise: his triumph is reflected from the faces of his hearers, and sounded in volleys from their lips.

It must be remembered that the oratory of a nation is a product of the national life. It is not a thing apart. There are periods in the history of every nation when we should expect the appearance of great orators, and there are other periods when great orators would be exceptional, if not impossible. Very little study of the question will show that great orators, like great poets, painters, and musicians, appear not singly but in groups. Two conditions are essential: (1) There must be the stir of popular life associated with free institutions. (2) There must be great vital questions clamoring for solution, questions that appeal not only to the statesman and the student, but to the merchant and the farmer as well.

In France, such a period was the French Revolution, with Mirabeau and Danton as its spokesmen. In England, the reign of George III witnessed the most splendid outbursts of eloquence yet recorded in English annals: Chatham, Pitt, Burke, Erskine, and Fox are names that would add lustre to the reign of any monarch and to the history of any country. In America, we have had two such periods: (1) The first was the Revolutionary Period, by which is meant the period immediately preceding and following the Revolutionary War. (2) The second may be said to begin with the year 1830, or with the presidency of Andrew Jackson, and to end with the year 1850. In the first period the leading questions at issue were (a) resistance to Great Britain and (b) the maintenance of popular freedom by means of a constitution in which the claims of the individual states might be harmonized with the powers of a strong central government. In the second period, the questions were, again, chiefly constitutional,—slavery, secession, the tariff, and nullification being debated by the giants of those days mainly as they were related to the Constitution of 1789. This time, however, oratory and statesmanship were alike powerless to avert the coming struggle, and the questions that Clay, Calhoun, and Webster wrestled with were de-

SOUTHERN ORATORY BEFORE THE WAR 85

stined, after their death, to be settled by the arbitrament of battle.

What part has the South played on the arena of political oratory? What laurels are hers? Without disparagement to any section of our common country I wish to say that in my opinion one of the most inspiring chapters in American history is yet to be written, and that chapter will be dedicated to Southern Oratory of the past. In all that constitutes true eloquence, in that subtle union of manly thought with impassioned utterance, the South can challenge comparison with any nation and with any age. Her skill in the council chamber and on the hustings has been equal to her daring on the field of battle. And the variety of her oratory is equal to its excellence. From the deep, sonorous sentences of Patrick Henry, the clear, incisive, bell-like tones of Calhoun, the defiant, impetuous, yet graceful periods of Henry Clay, to the prodigal wealth of thought, emotion, and imagination that flamed from the lips of Prentiss, there is not a note in the whole gamut of oratory which the South has not sounded and sounded with the ease of the master.

I shall mention only the leading names, selecting them in their chronological order. My purpose is more to call attention to the subject by outlining it than to exhaust it.

Patrick Henry
Washington
Madison
Jefferson
John Randolph.

Randolph lived long enough to read the accounts of the great debate between Daniel Webster and Robert Y. Hayne, of South Carolina, the most memorable contest which the Senate of the United States has ever witnessed. It took place, as is well known, in 1830, and was really the opening cannon of a struggle that was to end only when Lee laid down his sword on the field of Appomattox.

Every schoolboy knows the close of Webster's speech, "Liberty and Union, now and forever, one and inseparable." But how many know the eloquent conclusion of Hayne's second speech in reply: "The gentleman is for marching under a banner studded all over with stars, and bearing the inscription, 'Liberty and Union.' I had thought, Sir, the gentleman would have borne a standard displaying in its ample folds a brilliant sun, extending its golden rays from the center to the extremities, in the brightness of whose beams the 'little stars hide their diminished heads.' Ours, Sir, is the banner of the Constitution; the twenty-four stars are there in all their undiminished lustre; on it is inscribed, *'Liberty—the Constitution—Union.'* We offer up our fervent prayers to the Father of Mercies that it may continue to wave for ages yet to come over a Free, Happy, and United People."

It is not my purpose this morning to stir again the embers of this great debate, except in so far as I think injustice, or at least lack of justice, has been done to Mr. Hayne. I regret that time forbids my reading even a short extract from the famous speech to which Webster replied. Not even the most blinded partisan can claim that Mr. Hayne was the orator that Daniel Webster was. Nature had endowed Webster in this respect as she has endowed no other man born on this continent. "There goes a king" said a British day laborer on seeing Mr. Webster; and Thomas Carlyle wrote: "As a parliamentary Hercules one would incline to back him at first sight against all the extant world." When Webster was pointed out to Sydney Smith on the streets of London, the famous wit remarked: "He must be a fraud. No man can really be as great as he looks." The impression made by Webster's speech upon those who heard it was incontestably greater than the impression made by Mr. Hayne's speech. But it is not easy to see how any one can read the two speeches and claim that Webster answered Hayne. Opinions were divided at the time. A correspondent of the *Philadelphia Gazette* wrote, "I cannot admit the justice of Mr. Webster's reply, yet I can admire the force and ingenuity with which he urged them (his views)." And now after more than sixty years, Henry Cabot Lodge, of Massachusetts, in his *Life of Daniel Webster*, American Statesmen Series, frankly admits that, though Webster argued ably, eloquently, and ingeniously, the constitutional facts, as Hayne presented them, were unfortunately against him. The late Hamilton W. Mable said: "In the great debate Hayne spoke authoritatively for the framers of the constitution, while Webster spoke authoritatively for the necessities of the nation." "Hayne," writes Woodrow Wilson, "spoke for the past, Webster for the future." I need hardly remind you that the question at issue related solely to the past, to the meaning of a constitution made forty-three years before. In other words Webster was defeated on his own chosen field of constitutional interpretation.

Why, then, did Webster's speech produce such a profound impression throughout the country, especially in the North? Because, as Senator Lodge justly intimates, that speech gave expression to what many men had come to believe the government to be, and wished it to be. Secession seemed a much more terrible thing in 1830 than it did thirty or forty years earlier, when our government was still in a sort of experimental stage. Daniel Webster nobly portrayed the conception of the constitution entertained in the North and by some in the South. He crystallized this conception in clear and enduring shape, for it was admittedly the greatest speech of his life. But when he tried to answer Mr. Hayne's historical arguments, when he attempted to harmonize the Northern idea of the Constitution with the Constitution itself, made forty-three years before, and especially with the palpable meaning of the Kentucky and Virginia Resolutions of 1798, he attempted the impossible; and it does Senator Lodge credit that he so frankly admits it.

Mr. Hayne was by no means crushed by Webster's speech, as we so often hear it said. He was made Governor of South Carolina two years later and Wm. C. Preston, himself a consummate orator, said of his inaugural address: "It was the most successful display of eloquence I have ever heard. I was agitated and subdued under its influence; many wept from excitement, and all, of all parties, were borne away, entranced by the magic powers of the speaker."

I cannot refrain from giving an extract in this connection from the beautiful inscription which Mrs. Hayne caused to be engraved upon the tomb of her honored husband in Charleston, an inscription which the united testimony of friends declares no more than just: "It is the smitten heart that would relieve its anguish by this record of his rare virtues, his real nobleness, his incomparable excellence. That heart alone can know how far the wisdom of the Statesman, the eloquence of the Senator, and the courage of the Hero were transcended by those sublime qualities which made him the Idol of his Wife, the Pattern of his Children, the Guide of his Friends, the honest, incorruptible Patriot."

While this great debate was going on, there sat listening to it one who was destined three years later to enter the lists against Mr. Webster and to leave marks upon the great New Englander's armor which time would not soon wear away. I refer, of course, to the great champion of nullification John C. Calhoun. Calhoun was a ghostly looking man, erect, alert, and earnest, with hair standing up "Like quills upon the fretful porpentine." He had an eye as piercing as a hawk's. His cheeks were blanched by prolonged and intense study. His lips, "accurately closed," gave some hint of the invincible will and unalterable conviction that slumbered within. The sinewy intellect and merciless logic of the great nullifier, together with his unrivalled power of analysis, stand out upon every page of his speeches. He used few illustrations and became at times so abstract and metaphysical as not to be easily understood. Yet one who heard him frequently, though not sympathizing with his views, said that "His ideas were so clear and his language so plain that he made a path of light through any subject that he discussed." Calhoun has been anathematized more than any other

Southern statesman of the old regime, but the man is to be pitied who can study Calhoun's career and then doubt either the nobleness of his character or the splendor of his intellect. He seems to me the subtlest purely intellectual force that has applied itself to the problems of American statecraft since the founding of our government.

It is gratifying to read the following tribute to Calhoun from the pen of Mr. Oliver Dyer. He knew Calhoun well and had been taught to consider him as the incarnation of the Devil. Though Mr. Dyer was a Northern man and had no sympathy with the doctrine of nullification or secession, he is fair and frank enough to speak thus of the great champion of statesrights: "He (Calhoun) was so morally clean and spiritually pure that it was a pleasure to have one's soul get close to his soul—a feeling that I have never had for any other man. He seemed to exhale an atmosphere of purity as fresh and sweet and bracing as a breeze from the prairie, the ocean, or the mountain. . . . He was inexpressibly urbane, refined, gentle, winning. As I came to know him well, and saw his exquisitely beautiful nature mirrored in his face, his countenance no longer seemed Satanic, but angelic, and his benignant greeting in the morning was like a benediction that lasted the whole day."

Two other names must be mentioned, Seargeant Smith Prentiss and Henry Clay.

Such, then, is a sketch, and only a sketch, of some of the orators who lived and died before the first gun of civil war was fired, and whom the South is proud to claim as her jewels. If the limits of my subject permitted, I should call the roll of those other great orators, whose lives spanned the period of civil war, whose genius and courage upheld the traditions of a glorious past, and whose names and fames are so tenderly interwoven with the times that tried men's souls. I should speak of Benjamin H. Hill, of Alexander H. Stephens, of Robert Tombs, of Judah P. Benjamin, of Jefferson Davis, and of L. Q. C. Lamar. In spite of popular defamation, they lived the patriot's life and have entered upon the patriot's reward.

But I have tried only to outline my subject, and to suggest to the young men before me what a rich field of historical material is awaiting development at their hands. The speeches of the men whom I have mentioned, though their words were frequently turning points in state history and in national history, are almost inaccessible today. If you search for them, you must search in dusty, moth-eaten volumes, and along forgotten shelves. Men of the South, this should not be. The great orations of the past should be to us a heritage sacred and priceless.

SOUTHERN ORATORY BEFORE THE WAR

Never will our history be truly written till these dead voices are made to speak again. It is not enough that our fathers made history: we must write it, or it will remain unwritten. And when it is written, as written it will yet be, in truth and candor, it will be found that the South has not juggled with words merely to charm the fancy or to tickle the ears of her auditors. Far, far from it. Whenever oppression stalked through the land; whenever constitutional and civil rights felt the rude foot of the invader; whenever state liberty, which means personal liberty, seemed menaced by the encroachments of centralized power;—her voice has sounded the trumpet call to freedom and redress. It matters not that the verdict of history has in some cases gone against her: I do not claim that she was infallible, nor did she claim it; but I do claim—and I fling the challenge upon the open pages of my country's history—that her voice was raised never in behalf of conscious wrong, never in defence of known usurpation.

THOMAS JEFFERSON [1]

HAD THOMAS JEFFERSON not written the Declaration of Independence or had he written nothing but the Declaration of Independence, he would still have deserved a place in the history of American literature. As a writer Franklin surpassed him in simplicity of style. As a man Washington towers above him in sublimity of character. But as an exponent of democracy neither Franklin nor Washington compares with him in extent or permanence of influence. Of all the political philosophers that America has produced Thomas Jefferson is the profoundest. He has influenced not only political thought in its widest sense but almost every phase of American life. His voluminous writings have been several times arranged and published in topical divisions, so that the student of history or of literature can at once find out what Jefferson thought on every conceivable topic.[2] A mere *glance* at the variety of the topics about which Jefferson has

---

[1] The fourth lecture in a course in American literature given in German at the University of Berlin during the fall and winter of 1910-11. (Winter semester 1910-11.) The entire series was published in German under the title *Die Amerikanische Literatur*, the second volume in the *Bibliothek der Amerikanischen Kulturgeschichte*. Berlin 1912. (pp. 60-81).

[2] See *The Jefferson Cyclopedia*, by John P. Foley, N. Y., 1900, and *The Life and Writings of Thomas Jefferson*, by S. E. Forman, Indianapolis, 1900.

written is in itself an introduction to the early history of the United States; a *study* of these topics is a liberal education in the principles of self-government and in the inalienable rights of mankind.

Some idea of the range of Jefferson's thought may be gained from an enumeration of some of the topics that recur most frequently in his works. These are: agriculture, architecture, astronomy, Napoleon Bonaparte, George III, the dangers of centralization in government, true Christianity, the tests of good citizenship, the utility of Latin and Greek, the right pronunciation of Greek, the value of Anglo-Saxon or Old English as a college study, free commerce with all nations, the character of the Indians, the variety of Indian languages, universal education, religious and intellectual freedom, true friendship, journalism, history, Homer, music, negroes, Plato, and English prosody.

His chief interests, however, lay in the kindred domains of political freedom, religious freedom, and universal education. Though he was twice President of the United States, though he added nearly a million square miles to United States territory, he mentions none of these things in the inscription which he wrote to be placed upon his tomb. This reads as follows:

> Here was buried
> Thomas Jefferson
> Author of the
> Declaration
> of
> American Independence
> of the
> Statute of Virginia
> for
> Religious Freedom
> And Father of the
> University of Virginia.

In other words Jefferson's thought and his activities centered around the individual. Institutions, whether social, religious, or political, were to be tolerated only in so far as they gave freedom of development to the individual. He was also an idealist, as bold as Emerson but more practical. Individualism and idealism have been the dominant factors in American literature. Among those, therefore, who, directly or indirectly, have shaped the course of American literature, Thomas Jefferson deserves a foremost place.

He was born in Albemarle County, near Charlottesville, Virginia, April 13, 1743. His father was of Welsh descent, while his mother traced her ancestry back to the Scotch Earls of Murray. After receiving a preparatory training at home, Jefferson entered William and Mary College, in Virginia, a small institution founded in 1693. "It was my great good fortune," said Jefferson, speaking of his college days, "and what probably fixed the destinies of my life, that Dr. William Small of Scotland was then professor of mathematics, a man profound in most of the useful branches of science [knowledge], with a happy talent of communication, correct and gentlemanly manners, and an enlarged and liberal mind. He, most happily for me, became soon attached to me and made me his daily companion, when not engaged in the school; and from his conversation I got my first views of the expansion of science and of the system of things in which we are placed."

As Dr. Small was a skeptic, it may be well to give in Jefferson's own words the latter's religious views. To Dr. Benjamin Rush he wrote in 1803: "To the corruptions of Christianity I am indeed opposed; but not to the genuine precepts of Jesus himself. I am a Christian in the only sense He wished any one to be: sincerely attached to His doctrines in preference to all others, ascribing to Himself every human excellence and believing He never claimed any other." In other words Jefferson was from the beginning a Unitarian.

After graduating from William and Mary College in 1762 he entered at once upon the study of law. His notebook shows that he had a passion for tracing all legal forms back to their Anglo-Saxon origins. Indeed forms of all sorts were interesting to Jefferson only in so far as they embodied permanent traits of human nature or principles of philosophy. He criticized the Constitution of the United States because it contained no statement of universal human rights. It did not trace the principles of self-government far enough back.

When Jefferson went to Philadelphia in June 1775 as a member of Congress, his fame had preceded him. It was known that he could "calculate an eclipse, survey an estate, tie an artery, plan an edifice, try a cause, break a horse, dance a minuet, and play the violin." He also brought with him the reputation of a skillful writer. "Writings of his were handed about," says John Adams, "remarkable for the peculiar felicity of expression." It was no wonder, then, that the honor of drafting the Declaration of Independence fell to Jefferson. He spent about three weeks upon the task, sparing no pains to make the great document representative in thought and perfect in expression. The reception accorded the Declaration by the different colonies and its further effect upon political thought the world over stamp it as one of the greatest products of human effort. It differs from other documents of similar import in two important respects: first, it is eloquent. It is not a dry summary of grievances but is inspired by a burning zeal for liberty and justice. It touches the heart and quickens the pulse today as effectively as it did on that memorable fourth of July, when it voiced the new hopes and resolves of a new nation.

In the second place, it bases its appeals not on historical facts alone but on what Jefferson believed to be the eternal principles of right and justice. Edmund Burke had declared again and again that the American colonists were contending for liberties based not on metaphysical principles but on historical facts. The same views had been expressed many years before by Benjamin Franklin. Jefferson thought otherwise, and the after history of the Declaration has justified the view of its author. The strongest part of the great document is not the recital of special grievances, but rather the luminous statement of the rights of men in civil societies. It is this statement that stamps Jefferson as a political seer and prophet; it is this statement that is memorized by thousands of children in American schools; it is this statement that has made the Declaration not only a turning point in American history but an epoch in the history of liberty itself.

As a member of the Virginia General Assembly Jefferson succeeded, against great opposition, in abolishing the laws of entail and primogeniture, and in effecting the separation of Church and State. From 1779 to 1809 he served successively as Governor of Virginia, Member of Congress, Minister to France, Secretary of State, Vice President, and President.

"The succession to Franklin," said Jefferson, "at the Court of France, was an excellent school of humility. On being presented to any one as the Minister of America, the commonplace question used in such cases was: 'C'est vous, Monsieur, qui remplace le Docteur Franklin.' I generally answered: 'No one can replace him, Sir; I am only his successor.'" It may be remarked here that Jefferson considered Franklin's writings models of simple, clear English. He considered Bolingbroke's style the best modern illustration of "the lofty, rhythmical, full-flowing eloquence of Cicero."

When Jefferson retired from politics in 1809—a notable date in American history—he had founded a new party and dethroned an old one. This he did not by public speeches, nor by newspaper controversy, nor by social influence, but by writing private letters. Franklin numbered more correspondents in foreign lands, but Jefferson's pen was far more potent than Franklin's at home. Jefferson had also the advantage of a definite, clear-cut conception of government, a conception from which he never swerved.

The Federalists believed in a government by leaders, Jefferson in a government of the people, for the people, and by the people. The present democratic party is, of course, lineally descended from Jefferson but both parties invoke his authority today in every crisis and in every campaign. He is, in a word, not so much the founder of a distinct party striving for office and power as the voice of the people striving for personal freedom through political institutions.

The last seventeen years of his life spent in retirement at Monticello were the happiest of his whole career. "A part of my occupation," he writes to General Kosciusko in 1810, "and by no means the least pleasing, is the direction of the studies of such young men as ask it. They place themselves in the neighboring village and have the use of my library and counsel, and make a part of my society. In advising the course of their reading, I endeavor to keep their attention fixed on the main objects of all science, the freedom and happiness of man."

Jefferson's library contained doubtless the best collection of *Americana* in existence. When the Congressional library was burned by British troops in 1814, Jefferson's books were bought by the national government for the sum of $24,000. "While residing in Paris," says Jefferson in a letter to Mr. S. H. Smith, written in 1814, "I devoted every afternoon I was disengaged, for a summer or two, in examining all the principal book stores, turning over every book with my own hands, and putting by everything which related to America, and indeed whatever was rare and valuable in every science. Besides this, I had standing orders during the whole time I was in Europe, on its principal book-marts, particularly Amsterdam, Frankfort, Madrid, and London, for such works relating to America as could not be found in Paris."

The last years of Jefferson's life were devoted to founding the University of Virginia, to conducting his vast estate at Monticello, to correspondence, and to putting the finishing touches to certain writings begun long before. His plan of public education is that now adopted in every state of the Union. There were to be three stages: primary schools, secondary or high schools, and the college or university.[1] The University of Virginia was opened in the year 1825.[2] Jefferson died July 4, 1826. Among the students who entered the University in 1825 was Edgar Allan Poe. Perhaps the time will come when some gifted artist will sketch these two world figures as they met in social intercourse at Monticello or passed each other on the steps of the Rotunda. Such a painting would remind the beholder that the University was not only

---

[1] See Jefferson's *Notes on Virginia.*

[2] See *Thomas Jefferson and the University of Virginia,* by Herbert B. Adams. Washington, 1888.

the daughter of our greatest statesman but also the young mother of our greatest poet.

Jefferson's manysidedness stands out most clearly when we view him not in his favorite domain of law and government but rather as a keen observer and persistent investigator. To the end of his days he was a tireless student of men and things, of the past and the present. If individual liberty was his *Hauptfach*, all other subjects were his *Nebenfacher*. He believed, however, that a man should study first the things near at hand, that education, like charity, begins at home. It is not surprising, therefore, that his first published work, apart from political papers was a study of his native state.

His *Notes on Virginia* was prepared for the information of the French. It was written in 1781, corrected and enlarged in 1782, and privately printed in 1784. A French translation was published at Paris in 1786, a German translation at Leipzig (*Beschreibung von Virginien*) in 1789. The first London edition appeared in 1787. "This work," says G. Brown Goode, late Assistant Secretary of the Smithsonian Institution,[1] "was the first comprehensive treatise upon the topography, natural history, and natural resources of one of the United States, and was the precursor of the great library of scien-

---
[1] See "Jefferson as a Man of Science" (*Memorial Edition of Jefferson's Works*, vol. XIX. Washington 1904).

tific reports which have since been issued by the State and Federal governments. If measured by its influence it is the most important scientific work as yet published in America." This work contains also Jefferson's best writing from a purely literary point of view. His skill in description, his breadth and accuracy of observation, his poetic appreciation of natural scenery, the mingled pride and delight that he felt in making the beauties of Virginia known abroad, all combine to make this book significant in literature as well as in science.

In 1789 he completed a little work of thirty-seven octavo pages entitled *Thoughts on English Prosody*, a work not published until 1904.[1] The position taken by Jefferson, though not original with him, was worked out by him in his own way and remains today the accepted view. His purpose was to prove that English verse is not based, like Latin and Greek, upon long and short syllables but upon accent. "That the accent shall never be displaced from the syllable whereon usage hath established it is the fundamental law of English verse." Foreigners, he thinks, can learn the accent of English better from poetry than from prose or from the study of the dictionary. The second part of his treatise is devoted to line-lengths in poetry, a subject to which nothing fundamental has been added since Jefferson wrote.

---

[1] See in the *Memorial Edition*, vol. XVIII.

Jefferson's next publication marked the beginning of paleontology in the United States. The bones of an unknown quadruped had been discovered in Virginia and on March 10, 1797, Jefferson, at that time Vice-President of the United States, read before the American Philosophical Society *A Memoir on the Discovery of Certain Bones of a Quadruped of the Clawed Kind in the Western Parts of Virginia.* The paper was published in the *Transactions of the Philosophical Society*, volume IV, 1799. In 1801 it was translated into German and published (in Hoff's *Magazin fur die gesammte Mineralogie,* vol. I) as "Nachricht von Fossilen Colossalen Knochen eines Raubthieres in Virginien Gefunden." When Jefferson went to Philadelphia to be inaugurated Vice-President he took with him a collection of fossil bones for further study. In 1808, when the New England newspapers were denouncing him for his Embargo Act, he was carrying on paleontological investigations in an unfinished room of the White House where he had collected three hundred specimens of fossil bones. During his residence in Paris he kept Harvard, Yale, William and Mary College, and the College of Philadelphia informed of all that happened in the scientific circles of Europe.[1] It was only on account of age that he resigned in 1814 the presidency of the

---

[1] See "Jefferson as a Man of Science," by Cyrus Adler. *Memorial Edition*, vol. XIX, p. v.

American Philosophical Society which he had held since 1797.

In October 1798, the month and year in which he drafted the famous Kentucky Resolutions, Jefferson sends to Herbert Croft, London, a manuscript copy of *An Essay on Anglo-Saxon and Modern Dialects of the English Language*. In the letter accompanying the manuscript he writes as follows: "I was led to set a due value on the study of the Northern [Germanic] languages, and especially of our Anglo-Saxon, while I was a student of the law, by being obliged to recur to that source for explanation of a multitude of law-terms. . . . I accordingly devoted some time to its study, but my busy life has not permitted me to indulge in a pursuit to which I felt great attraction. While engaged in it, however, some ideas occurred for facilitating the study by simplifying its grammar. . . . Some of these ideas I noted at the time on the blank leaves of my Elstob's *Anglo-Saxon Grammar*. . . . Thinking that I cannot submit those ideas to a better judge than yourself, and that if you find them of any value you may put them to some use, either as hints in your dictionary or in some other way, I will copy them as a sequel to this letter."

The *Essay on Anglo-Saxon* was first published by the University of Virginia in 1851. It is reprinted in the *Memorial Edition of Jefferson's Works*, vol.

XVIII, 1904. The work contains 47 octavo pages and treats its subject under four divisions: Alphabet, Orthography, Pronunciation, and Grammar. It is a remarkable little grammar from whatever view point we consider it. It was not only the first treatise of its kind to appear on this side of the water but is marked throughout by originality of treatment. Jefferson does not blindly copy his English authorities but throws out many valuable and ingenious suggestions for the teacher. He thinks that Hickes and Bosworth have treated Old English too much from the standpoint of Latin and Greek—an opinion that time has sanctioned.

About the year 1819 Jefferson completed a work called *The Life and Morals of Jesus of Nazareth, extracted textually from the Gospels in Greek, Latin, French, and English*. It is commonly known as Jefferson's Bible. The publication of this work by the National Government in 1904 aroused a storm of opposition. Jefferson's original idea was to narrate the life and teachings of Christ in simple extracts from the four Gospels for the use of the Indians, to whom, he thought, the simpler form would appeal. But he abandoned this idea and prepared a little volume solely for his own use. He believed that the four Gospels contained much that Christ did not say or do. He wished to separate the chaff from the wheat. "There will be found remaining," he writes to John

Adams (October 12, 1813), "the most sublime and benevolent code of morals which has ever been offered to man." This little volume was Jefferson's constant companion during his declining years. "I never go to bed," he writes to Dr. Vine Utley, "without an hour or a half hour's previous reading of something moral whereon to ruminate in the intervals of sleep." The volume most often in his hands at such times was his own book of Bible selections.

Jefferson's *Autobiography* seems to have been written between January 6 and July 29, 1821. It ends with the year 1790. It is not one of the great autobiographies, partly because it deals almost wholly with things political and partly because it is written as a contribution to history rather than to literature.[1] It suffers in comparison with Franklin's *Autobiography* because the purpose of the two men was wholly different and also because Jefferson had little or no sense of humor. The work is dignified, learned, indispensable to the historian of Virginia or of the United States, but not generally interesting. Jefferson's real autobiography is written in the Declaration

---

[1] A continuation of the *Autobiography* is found in the volume of *Anas* which contains among other things all the official opinions given by Jefferson as Secretary of State to President Washington. The period covered is 1791-1806. As Jefferson's "Explanation" or Preface is dated 1818 I am inclined to think that the *Autobiography* was planned merely as a sort of Introduction to the *Anas*. This would account for its impersonal character.

of Independence, in his extracts from the Bible, and in his letters.

Dr. Samuel Johnson has somewhere told of a man who carried a brick in his pocket as a specimen of the architecture of a certain house which he wished to sell. To attempt in the few minutes at my disposal to illustrate the range of Jefferson's thought and the nature of his style by a few extracts from his voluminous correspondence is to incur, I fear, an analogous reproach. The extracts, however, will be made with a view chiefly to showing Jefferson's attitude toward language and literature. Such extracts are interesting and significant not merely because they embody Jefferson's own views but because his views have been more potent than those of any other man of his time in moulding public opinion in America.

He did not believe that the attempt to reform English spelling would be successful. "It would be a step gained in the progress of general reformation, if it could prevail. But—judging of the future by the past, I expect no better fortune to this than similar preceding propositions have experienced. . . . Time alone insensibly wears down old habits and produces small changes at long intervals, and to this process we must all accommodate ourselves. Our Anglo-Saxon ancestors had twenty ways of spelling the word 'many.' Ten centuries have dropped all of them and substituted that which we now use."[1]

He believed that grammar was made for man and not man for grammar. "Where strictness of grammar does not weaken expression, it should be attended to . . . . But where by small grammatical negligences, the energy of an idea is condensed, or a word stands for a sentence, I hold grammatical rigor in contempt."[2]

Twenty-two years later he writes: "I am not a friend to a scrupulous purism of style. I readily sacrifice the niceties of syntax to euphony and strength. It is by boldly neglecting the rigorisms of grammar that Tacitus has made himself the strongest writer in the world. The hyperesthetics call him barbarous; but I should be sorry to exchange his barbarisms for their wire-drawn purisms. Some of his sentences are as strong as language can make them . . . . To explain my meaning of an English example, I will quote the motto of one of the regicides of Charles I: 'Rebellion *to* tyrants is obedience to God.' Correct its syntax, 'Rebellion *against* tyrants is obedience to God;' it has lost all the strength and beauty of the antithesis."[3]

---

[1] To John Wilson, 1813.
[2] To James Madison, 1801.
[3] To Edward Everett, 1823.

He was especially interested in the history of the English language. He hoped to see the study of Anglo-Saxon made "a regular part of our common English education."[1] At his suggestion it was introduced into the first curriculum of the University of Virginia, long before it was studied elsewhere in America. "The cultivation of Anglo-Saxon," he writes, in 1825, "is a hobby which too often runs away with me when I meant not to give the rein. Our youth seem disposed to mount it with me, and to begin their course where mine is ended."[2]

He believed in having a standard of written and spoken English but was one of the first to see the real significance of dialects. "It is much to be wished that the publication of the present county dialects of England should go on. It will restore to us our language in all its shades of variation. . . . We shall find in Shakespeare new sublimities which we had never tasted before and find beauties in our ancient poets which are lost to us now."[3] He saw clearly that the introduction of new words into English was an evidence of growth rather than of decay. "I have been not a little disappointed and made suspicious of my own judgment on seeing the Edinburgh Reviewers, the ablest critics of the age, set their faces

---
[1] To J. Evelyn Denison, 1825.
[2] To J. Evelyn Denison, 1825.
[3] To J. Evelyn Denison, 1825.

against the introduction of new words into the English language; they are particularly apprehensive that the writers of the United States will adulterate it. Certainly so great and growing a population, spread over such an extent of country, with such a variety of climates, of productions, of arts, must enlarge their language to make it answer its purpose of expressing all ideas, the new as well as the old. The new circumstances under which we are placed call for new words, new phrases, and for the transfer of old words to new objects. . . . But will these adulterate or enrich the English language? Has the beautiful poetry of Burns or his Scottish dialect disfigured it? Did the Athenians consider the Doric, the Ionian, the Æolic, and other dialects as disfiguring or as beautifying their language?"[1]

In other words, Jefferson was not only an appreciative reader of ancient and modern literature but a scientific student of language for its own sake. At the age of seventy he writes a critique of Buttmann's *Griechische Grammatik*, translated by Everett, and endeavors to show that the author is wrong in denying an ablative case to Greek.[2] He wishes to study Gaelic so that he may read the *Poems of Ossian* in the original.[3] With prophetic vision he urged upon

---
[1] To John Waldo, 1813.
[2] To Edward Everett, 1823.
[3] To Charles McPherson, 1773.

Americans the importance of studying Spanish. "Bestow great attention on the Spanish language, and endeavor to acquire an accurate knowledge of it. Our future connections with Spain and Spanish America will render that language a valuable acquisition."[1]

To a mind like Jefferson's the varieties of Indian tribes and languages in America opened a rare opportunity for original investigation. "I believe the Indian to be in body and mind," he writes, "equal to the white man."[2] It was his opinion that only in the study of the Indian language lay the clue to the origin of the Indian race and the explanation of Indian tribal affinities. "I have through the course of my life availed myself of every opportunity of procuring vocabularies of the languages of every Indian tribe which either myself or my friends could have access to. They amounted to about forty, more or less perfect. But in their passage from Washington to Monticello the trunk in which they were was stolen and plundered, and some fragments only of the vocabularies were recovered."[3]

But Jefferson's realization of the value and worth of language study, apart from its service as an introduction to literature, is best shown in his comments on a Cherokee grammar, which a friend had sent

---
[1] To Peter Carr, 1787.
[2] To General Chastellux, 1785.
[3] To Mr. Duponceau, 1817.

him. "Your Cherokee grammar," he writes,[1] "I have gone over with attention and satisfaction. We generally learn languages for the benefit of reading the books written in them. But here our reward must be the addition made to the philosophy of language." It is in words like these that Jefferson's superiority in mental outlook to his great contemporary, Benjamin Franklin, is most clearly shown. Franklin would hardly have conceded the importance of studying Cherokee grammar if there was no Cherokee literature; nor do I think he would have admitted that there is any philosophy in the language spoken by the Cherokees or by any other uncivilized Indian tribe. In advocating learning for the sake of learning, science for the sake of science, Jefferson was a pioneer among his American contemporaries.

Jefferson never lost faith in the doctrine of the absolute freedom of the press, though few men were vilified as he was by partisan newspapers. "When the press is free," he writes,[2] "and every man able to read, all is safe." And again: "The only security of all is in a free press. The force of public opinion cannot be resisted, when permitted freely to be expressed. The agitation it produces must be submitted to. It is necessary to keep the waters pure."[3] "Were

---
[1] To _____ 1825. See *The Writings of Thomas Jefferson*, edited by H. A. Washington, 1833-1854, vol. VII, p. 399.

[2] To Charles Yancey, 1816.

[3] To Marquis de LaFayette, 1823.

it left to me to decide," he writes in a memorable letter,[1] "whether we should have a government without newspapers, or newspapers without a government, I should not hesitate a moment to prefer the latter."

In his later years Jefferson came to distrust the information found in newspapers and had recourse to his favorite Latin and Greek authors. "Nothing can now be believed," he writes[2] in 1807, "which is seen in a newspaper." "I have given up newspapers in exchange for Tacitus and Thucydides, for Newton and Euclid, and find myself much the happier."[3] "I never in my life," he writes again, "directly or indirectly, wrote one sentence for a newspaper."[4]

In regard to history in general, one may trace in Jefferson's letters an increasing preference for ancient history rather than modern and for original sources rather than mere compilations. "I am happier while reading the history of ancient than of modern times. . . . The total banishment of all moral principle from the code which governs the intercourse of nations . . . sickens my soul unto death."[5] "In all cases I prefer original authors to compilers."[6]

---
[1] To Edward Carrington, 1787.
[2] To John Norvell, 1807.
[3] To John Adams, 1812.
[4] The *Anas*, 1800.
[5] To William Duane, 1813.
[6] To _____ 1925. See *The Writings of Thomas Jefferson*, edited by H. A. Washington, 1853-1854, vol. VII, p. 411.

The history of the American Revolution Jefferson believed could never be truly written. "Who can write it? Nobody, except merely its external facts; all its councils, designs, and discussions having been conducted by Congress with closed doors, and with no members, as far as I know, having even made notes of them."[1] A few years later he thought that the earlier history of the United States might be collected from private letters. "The opening scenes of our present government will not be seen in their true aspect until the letters of the day, now held in private hoards, shall be broken up and laid open to public view."[2]

In his early years Jefferson was passionately fond of poetry and prose fiction. In a letter written when he was twenty-eight years of age, he states with great clearness and with many apt illustrations the fundamental difference between history and fiction as educational agencies. "I appeal to every reader of feeling and sentiment whether the fictitious murder of Duncan by Macbeth, in Shakespeare, does not excite in him as great a horror of villainy as the real one of Henry IV by Ravaillac . . . . A lively and lasting sense of filial duty is more effectually impressed on the mind of a son or daughter by reading *King Lear* than by all the dry volumes of ethics and

---

[1] To John Adams, 1815.
[2] To William Johnson, 1823.

divinity that ever were written. This is my idea of well written romance, of tragedy, comedy, and epic poetry."[1]

About the year 1801, however, he seems to have lost for a time all appreciation of poetry. The following passage is strikingly like the better known passage in which Darwin[2] bewails a similar defect of interest: "To my own mortification . . . of all men living I am the last who should undertake to decide as to the merits of poetry. In earlier life I was fond of it, and easily pleased. But as age and cares advanced, the powers of fancy have declined. Every year seems to have plucked a feather from her wings, till she can no longer waft me to those sublime heights to which it is necessary to accompany the poet. So much has my relish for poetry deserted me that, at present, I cannot read even Virgil with pleasure."[3] But after his retirement from political life his love of Latin poetry returned, and Horace, not Virgil, became his daily companion.[4]

It is needless to make further citations. Jefferson is still popularly known both at home and abroad chiefly as a statesman, as the author of the Declaration of Independence, and as a former President of

---
[1] To Robert Skipwith, 1771.
[2] See *Charles Darwin: Autobiography and Letters*, edited by his son Francis Darwin, 1893, pp. 53-54.
[3] To John D. Burke, 1801.
[4] See letter to David Howell, 1810, and to James Monroe, 1823.

the United States. He deserves to be known as a pioneer in almost the whole realm of scientific and humanistic thought. He influenced the course of American literature not only by the vigor of this style but because he looked at every problem from the viewpoint of individual freedom. No man that ever lived thought so persistently and so profoundly about democracy as Thomas Jefferson, but democracy was to him only another name for the freedom of the individual.

The late Senator George F. Hoar, of Massachusetts, commenting upon the range of Jefferson's influence, spoke as follows:[1] "If we want a sure proof of Thomas Jefferson's greatness, it will be found in the fact that men of every variety of political opinion, however far asunder, find confirmation of their doctrine in him. Every party in this country today reckons Jefferson as its patron saint. In my youth the political abolitionists made appeals to Jefferson the burden of their song. In the late discussion, which rent the country, about the Philippine Islands, one side quoted what Jefferson said in the Declaration of Independence, and the other what they thought he did in the acquisition of Louisiana. I do not know of any other American of whom this is true, unless it be that the different schools of theology and

---

[1] See "Special Introduction to the Writings of Thomas Jefferson," *Memorial Edition*, vol. I.

ethics seem inclined to do the same thing just now as to Ralph Waldo Emerson."

The mention of Emerson's name is suggestive. Emerson and Jefferson are the two greatest American exponents of individualism. But since the Civil War individualism as a principle of politics has steadily lost ground; as a principle of literature it has as steadily gained ground. Jeffersonianism is today better exemplified in American literature than in American politics.

EDGAR ALLAN POE [1]

POE is the necromancer of American literature. Read his prose and you crown him as the king of terror. Read his poetry and you concede a witchery of words found in no other of our American poets. There have been those who denied him a place among our greatest prose writers as well as our greatest poets; but no one has denied his power, his ability to reach the hidden places of the soul, his unique position in literature. No other poet has ever written so little and yet lodged so much in the memory as Poe. The emotions to which he appeals are neither many nor varied, but they are elemental and universal; and he appeals to them with a directness, with a weird vividness, with an impassioned intensity that have made him—though dead —a living force.

But the popular conception of the man's real service remains strangely vague. As a poet there are thousands of Americans who still think of him only as "the jingle man"; and as a prose writer they consider him chiefly a "manufacturer of cold creeps and maker of shivers." If this were all, his international fame would be not only hard to explain, but a stinging indictment of the literary taste of two worlds.

[1] Reprinted from *The Mentor*, September, 1922.

As I see it, Poe has influenced world literature in several definite ways. He had his weaknesses both of character and of genius. But America has produced no other genius whose life has been so mercilessly probed, whose every word and act has been so publicly blazoned, or whose motives have been so relentlessly scrutinized.

Poe has been a discoverer in the realm of meter and rhythm. I say "discoverer" advisedly, not "inventor." Men do not invent new rhyme combinations or new stanza forms. These forms were already existent, waiting for someone to call them into service. Now, Poe was a ceaseless experimenter in sound combinations, line combinations, and stanza combinations. His mastery of the technical devices of "repetition" and "parallelism" has permanently enriched the resources of English poetry. Take also the matter of new stanza forms. So far as I know, no new stanza had been coined in English literature since Spenser's time, till Poe appeared. The stanza structure of *The Raven,* of *To Helen,* and of *Ulalume* are altogether new creations. It was instantly recognized that Poe had done a new thing in these poems. Indeed, Poe gave such flexibility and malleableness to stanza structure as to justify us in saying of him that he found the stanza a *solid,* but left it a *liquid.* Then, too, his rhyme combinations, especially his characteristic blending of tripping syllables with sonorous syllables, as "napping" and "rapping" with "door" and "more," *Lenore* and *Evermore,* added appreciably to the gamut of poetic effects. No other poet of his time revealed so many unknown resources in poetic technique as Poe. "Poe has proved himself," says Edmund Gosse, "to be the Pied Piper of Hamelin to all later English poets. From Tennyson to Austin Dobson there is hardly one whose verse-music does not show traces of Poe's influence." Some are actually imitative of Poe.

Both in theory and practice Poe is the founder of the American short story as distinguished from the story that is merely short. His constructive leadership in this realm is recognized both at home and abroad. Washington Irving may be said to have legendized the short story, making it a means of storing legendary material in more enduring and attractive form. Hawthorne allegorized it, converting it into a sort of miniature *Pilgrim's Progress*. Bret Harte localized it, and California became the first romantic region that was lifted into literature on the shoulders of the short story. Joel Chandler Harris folklorized it with the Uncle Remus stories. O. Henry socialized it, leaving it the most flexible and responsive medium of expression of every day life and the social reaction that American literature has to its credit. Poe's contribution was unlike any of these. He retold no legends, he looked askance at allegory, he brought no locality into literature, he saw no career for art in folklore, and he found his creative inspiration not in the changing moods and whims of society about him, but in the visions and questionings deep within the human consciousness. His central contribution to the new form was not content, but structure. Poe *standardized* the short story; that is, he formulated a code for short-story writing that has been followed consciously or unconsciously in all lands. The old way was to begin with your chief character or your plot or your background, and to make one of these central and distinctive. But Poe declared that all of these should be made dependent upon and convergent upon the effect that you wish to produce—the *effect*, that was the chief thing.

Begin with this predetermined effect—that should be your real and only goal. Character, plot, and background have no reason for existence except as they contribute to this central and controlling purpose.

Poe's phrase, "totality of effect," sums up admirably his point of view. It was a formula from which he never swerved a hair's breadth. There are no unnecessary phrases or lines in his best stories. From the first word the lines begin to converge toward the predetermined and prearranged effect. In all lands his stories have been fruitful of suggestion, not because they brought a new message, but because they showed a faultless method of expressing whatever a writer of narrative had to say. There is no better model than that established by Poe. His motto was not merely brevity, but brevity plus effectiveness.

An old question, and a large one, in art is: Does genius act spontaneously or self-consciously? Poe stands for conscious and painstaking craftsmanship. Kant said that genius is wholly unconscious of its own operations. My own opinion is that Poe is much nearer the ultimate truth in this matter than Kant. At any rate, when Poe wrote his *Philosophy of Composition* (1846), telling just how he composed *The Raven,* he touched a big thought in a vital way and furnished the chief whetstone on which foreign critics, whether with him or against him, have sharpened their critical knives. He was thus a constructive force not only by what he did, *but by what he said as to how he did it*. He once called this self-attentiveness "a curse"; but, if it was a curse to him, it has been a blessing to other craftsmen. Arthur Ransome, the English critic, in his recent *Life of Poe,* says that what Poe called in himself a "curse" is the quality "that is at the bottom of all public knowledge of technique. The man who is as interested in the *way* of doing a thing as in the *thing when done* is the man who is likely to put a new tool into the hands of his fellow craftsmen." Poe's *Phi-*

losophy of Composition remains the best document in evidence to prove that genius, while unconscious perhaps in its larger inspirations, is not unconscious in its choice of technique to express itself. A study of the life and work of Leonardo da Vinci, Goethe, Sir Joshua Reynolds, Robert Louis Stevenson, Tennyson, or even Robert Burns will show the same sort of self-attentiveness. But Poe wrote with a freedom and minuteness of detail about the composition of his own work, that have made him preëminently the spokesman of those who believe that genius, whether in literature, painting, sculpture, or music, must toil painstakingly and self-consciously to bridge the chasm between the first rapture and the well-ordered expression of the rapture in concrete form.

H. H. Ewers, another recent biographer of Poe, observes that "Poe was the first poet to speak so plainly of his own work. In this respect he is distinctly American, and stands also on the very threshold of modern thought." You notice that Ewers tries to find in Poe something "distinctively American." Poe was the first American whose work suggested a new and sounder attitude toward the meaning of "Americanism." This was one of Poe's unconscious services, but none the less a real one. There was a time (it is with us yet) when critics thought that no writer could be American who did not embody in his work American history, American scenery, American geography, American traditions, or American characters. I hope that day is passing. I am convinced at least that it will pass and that it will pass *via* a right appreciation of what Poe has done. Nationalism is not physical, but spiritual and temperamental. It is to be seen in the extent to which a writer expresses and illustrates the *essential characteristics* of his people, and not by actual descriptions of national scenes, characters, and events in his writings, nor by "local color" of any kind. Byron and Browning are unmistakably English, though there is little or no English history or geography in their work. For at least thirty years foreign critics have been trying to appraise Poe in terms of a distinctively American product. Formerly they declared that he was utterly un-American, not only in theme, but also in essential genius. The changed attitude is significant. It means not only that Poe is being better understood but that he is the means by which America and Americanism are being better understood. To my mind Poe's Americanism lies not in his themes or in his geography—which are not American—but in his constructive genius. He thought in terms of structure. He is to be classed among our great builders. The very essence of Americanism is constructiveness. We have been builders ever since we landed on this continent. Poe's Americanism is found, then, in the conscious adaptation of means to end, in the quick realization of structural possibilities, in the practical handling of details, in the efficiency and effectiveness of his technique, which enabled him to body forth his visions in enduring forms, and even to originate the only new type of prose literature that our country has produced.

Let us think of Poe, then, not as some strange, abnormal being, ill-starred and ineffective. Let us think of him as one who, suffering much, thought much and wrought much; one who enlarged the realm of poetry by enriching and diversifying the range of poetic effect; one who touched the short story to finer issues in all lands; one who revealed the secret of poetic achievement as it had never been revealed before; and one who not only carried our common Americanism to the utmost bounds of civilization, but who also enriched the concept and idea of Americanism by a constructive genius still unparalleled in our literature.

JOEL CHANDLER HARRIS: A DISCUSSION OF THE NEGRO AS LITERARY MATERIAL[1]

IN THE FIRST lecture delivered in this course the statement was made that *Uncle Remus: his Songs and his Sayings* (1880), by Joel Chandler Harris, was "the most important single contribution to American Literature before 1870." Apart from its purely literary value, *Uncle Remus* has other claims upon our interest. Its significance, in fact, is fourfold: 1. In the character of Uncle Remus the author has done more than add a new figure to literature; he has typified a race and thus perpetuated a civilization. 2. In the stories told by Uncle Remus the author has brought the folk-tales of the negro into literature and thus laid the foundation for the scientific study of negro folk-lore. His work has, therefore, a purely historical and ethnological value not possessed by any other volume of short stories in American literature. 3. In the language spoken by Uncle Remus, the author has reproduced a dialect so completely and so accurately that each story is worth studying as marking a stage in the development of primitive English. 4. In the knowledge of negro

---

[1] The fourteenth lecture in a course in American Literature given in German at the University of Berlin during the winter semester 1910-11. The German lectures were published under the title *Die Amerikanische Literatur.*

JOEL CHANDLER HARRIS 129

life and the sympathy with negro character shown in the Uncle Remus stories there is suggested a better method for the solution of the negro problem in America than can be found in all the political platforms or merely legal enactments that American statesmanship has yet devised.

The life of Joel Chandler Harris was comparatively uneventful. He was born in Eatonton, Putnam County, Georgia, December 9, 1849. It is a remarkable fact that the middle counties of Georgia have produced the most representative humorists of the South. Among those who were born or who at some time lived in this part of Georgia may be mentioned A. B. Longstreet, the author of *Georgia Scenes*, Richard Malcolm Johnston, the author of *The Dukesborough Tales*, William Tappan Thompson, the author of *Major Jones's Courtship*, and Harry Stillwell Edwards,[1] the author of *Two Runaways and Other Stories*. In the same section were born the two poets Francis O. Ticknor, author of *Little Giffen of Tennessee*, and Sidney Lanier.

Middle Georgia was also before the war the most democratic part of the slave-holding states, a circumstance not without its influence upon the development of Harris's genius. "The sons of the richest men,"

---

[1] For biographical sketches of these writers and abstracts from their works, see the *Library of Southern Literature*.

he tells us,[2] "were put in the fields to work side by side with the negroes, and were thus taught to understand the importance of individual effort that leads to personal independence. It thus happened that there was a cordial and even an affectionate understanding between the slaves and their owners, that perhaps had no parallel elsewhere. The poorer whites had no reason to hold their heads down because they had to work for their living. The richest slave owners did not feel themselves above those who had few negroes or none. When a man called his neighbor 'Colonel,' or 'Judge,' it was to show his respect, nothing more. For the rest, the humblest held their heads as high as the richest, and were as quick, perhaps quicker, in a quarrel."

Young Harris owed little to the schools but much to a country printing office and to a large library in which it was his privilege to browse at will. At the age of twelve he read one morning the announcement that a new newspaper, *The Countryman*, was to be started a few miles from Eatonton. The editor, a Mr. Turner, the owner of a large plantation and many slaves, was a man of sound but old-fashioned literary taste and wished his paper to be modeled after *The Spectator* of Addison and Steele. This announcement kindled the ambition of young Harris who was already fa-

---
[2] See *Stories of Georgia*, by Joel Chandler Harris (N. Y., 1896), p. 241. This chapter is devoted to *Georgia Wit and Humor*.

miliar with the best literature of Queen Anne's time and to whom the very name *Spectator* recalled days and nights of indescribable delight. He applied at once for the vacant position of office boy, received a favorable answer from Mr. Turner, and devoted the rest of his life to journalism in his native State. The duties of his new position were not onerous and he found time, or took time, to hunt foxes, coons, opossums, and rabbits whenever he wished and to make himself familiar with every nook and corner of the surrounding country.

It was in these early years that Harris laid the foundation for his future work. There was not a negro myth or legend in which he was not interested; there was not a negro custom or peculiarity that he did not know; and there was not a sound or idiom of the negro language that he could not reproduce. "No man who has ever written," says Thomas Nelson Page, "has known one-tenth part about the negro that Mr. Harris knows, and for those who hereafter shall wish to find not merely the words but the real language of the negro of that section and the habits of mind of all American negroes of the old time, his works will prove the best thesaurus." In addition to his interest in the life about him Harris soon came to have an equal interest in Mr. Turner's large library. Among his favorite books were the writings of Sir Thomas Browne, the essays of Addison and Steele, and later the Bible and Shakespeare. His best loved writer, however, from first to last, and the one whose genius was most like his own, was Goldsmith. "The only way to describe my experience with *The Vicar of Wakefield*," he said in his later years, "is to acknowledge that I am a crank. It touches me more deeply, it gives me the 'all-overs' more severely than all others. Its simplicity, its air of extreme wonderment, have touched and continue to touch me deeply."

Among the writers of New England Harris seems to have cared least for Emerson and most for Lowell. "Culture," he wrote,[1] "is a very fine thing, indeed, but it is never of much account, either in life or in literature, unless it is used as a cat uses a mouse, as a source of mirth and luxury. It is at its finest in this country when it is grafted on the sturdiness that has made the nation what it is, and when it is fortified by the strong common sense that has developed and preserved the republic. This is culture with a definite aim and purpose . . . and we feel the ardent spirit of it in pretty much everything Mr. Lowell has written."

In his march through Georgia, General Sherman's army devastated the Turner plantation, and *The Countryman* was of course discontinued. After various experiences with different newspapers Harris joined

---

[1] See sketch of Harris in *Southern Writers* by William Malone Baskerville, vol. I, p. 13.

JOEL CHANDLER HARRIS 133

the staff of the *Atlanta Constitution* in 1876. At this time he was known chiefly as the writer of essays and poems,[1] but he began almost immediately to publish some of the plantation legends that he had heard from the lips of the negroes before and during the war. The first volume of these stories, *Uncle Remus: his Songs and his Sayings, the Folk-Lore of the Old Plantation*, was published in 1880. It contained thirty-four plantation legends or negro folk-tales, a few plantation proverbs, a story of the war, and twenty-one sayings or opinions of Uncle Remus, all being narrated by Uncle Remus himself. In 1883 appeared *Nights with Uncle Remus: Myths and Legends of the Old Plantation*. This contained sixty-nine new legends and was prefaced by an interesting introduction.[2] Among the new legends were a few told by Daddy Jake, a representative of the dialect spoken on the coastal rice plantations of South Carolina and

---

[1] See James Wood Davidson's *Living Writers of the South* (N. Y., 1869), p. 237. Thomas E. Watson wrote recently: "To my mind he (Harris) never did any better work than the poems and fugitive pieces which appeared long before the day of Uncle Remus." These were contributed chiefly to *The Morning News*, of Savannah, of which William Tappan Thompson was editor. There is urgent need that these fugitive contributions and those appearing in the *Atlanta Constitution* from 1876 to 1880 be collected and republished.

[2] Harris was too modest to call himself an ethnologist or even a serious student of folk-lore. See his humorous remarks about the above mentioned introduction in *The Late Mr. Watkins of Georgia*, one of the stories in *Tales of the Home Folks in Peace and War* (1898).

Georgia. These two volumes represent the author's best work in the domain of negro dialect and folklore, and were accorded instant recognition at home and abroad as opening a new and deeply interesting field both to literature and ethnology. Among Harris's later works may be mentioned *Uncle Remus and his Friends* (1892), *Mr. Rabbit at Home* (1895), *The Tar-Baby Story and Other Rhymes of Uncle Remus* (1904), *Told by Uncle Remus* (1905), *Uncle Remus and Brer Rabbit* (1907), together with numerous stories of the war and of the so-called reconstruction period that followed.

Just one year before his death he founded the *Uncle Remus's Magazine,* now known as *Uncle Remus's the Home Magazine.* Immediately after his death in 1908 the Uncle Remus Memorial Association was formed, the purpose of which is to purchase the home of the writer of the Uncle Remus stories, near Atlanta, Georgia, and to convert it into a suitable memorial. The name of the house is "The Sign of the Wren's Nest," because year after year a pair of wrens built their nest in the mail-box that hung at the gate. A member of the family protested against the daily inconvenience that the wrens occasioned, but the father would not let them be harmed. "Let them alone," he said, "we can make other arrangements for the letters." And so year after year the wrens built in the mail-box, the rabbits play in the yard, the mocking-birds sing from the shrubbery, and "Old Sis Cow" chews her cud under the shade of the trees.

"And many a moon
  Will wax and wane
Before we see
  His like again.

"The rabbit will hide
  As he always hid,
And the fox will do
  As he always did;

"But who will tell us
  What they say
Since Uncle Remus
  Has passed away?"

The significance of Uncle Remus as a study in negro character can best be brought out by a comparison of Harris's work with that of others, especially his predecessors, in the same field. The negroes themselves, by the way, can show at least two prose-writers and one poet of merited eminence. These are Booker T. Washington, W. E. Burghardt DuBois, and the late Paul Lawrence Dunbar. *Up from Slavery* (1901) by Washington and *The Souls of Black Folk* (1903) by DuBois are works of almost diametrically opposite styles. The former makes its appeal by its simplicity and restraint; the latter by its emotionalism and lack of restraint. Neither author, however, is of unmixed negro blood, and neither has come as close to the heart of his race as did Dunbar, a pure negro, in his *Lyrics of Lowly Life* (1896). He was the first American negro of pure African descent "to feel the negro life æsthetically and to express it lyrically."[1] His dialect poems, it may be added, are better than the poems that he wrote in standard English. Indeed Dunbar's command of correct English was always somewhat meager and uncertain.

Negro writers, however, were not the first to put their own race into literature or to realize the value of their own folk-lore. "The possibilities of negro folk-lore," says a recent negro writer,[2] "have carried it across the line, so that it has had strong influence on the work of such Southern writers as Thomas Nelson Page and Frank L. Stanton, and on that of George W. Cable. Its chief monument so far has been in the Uncle Remus tales of Brer Rabbit and Brer Fox told by Joel Chandler Harris."

The chief writers who preceded Harris in the attempt to portray negro character were William Gilmore Simms, Edgar Allan Poe, Harriet Beecher

---

[1] See introduction written by William Dean Howells to *Lyrics of Lowly Life* (1896).

[2] See Benjamin Griffith Brawley's *The Negro in Literature and Art* (Atlanta, Georgia, 1910), p. 5.

Stowe, Stephen Collins Foster, and Irwin Russell. Hector, the negro slave, in Simms's *Yemasse* (1835) and Jupiter in Poe's *Gold-Bug* (1843) are alike in many respects. Both belong to the type of faithful body servant,[1] both are natives of the coastal region of South Carolina, both illustrate a primitive sort of humor, and both speak an anglicized form of the Gullah (Gulla) dialect. Of the two, Hector is the better portrayed. His refusal (in chapter 49) to accept freedom when it is offered to him by his owner is by no means surprising; it is an evidence rather of Simms's familiarity with negro character and a reminder of the anomalous position in which a freedman in those days found himself.[2] Neither Hector nor Jupiter, however, can be said to have any individuality of his own. They are mere types, not individuals. Apart from their masters they have no separate existence at all.

The best known negro character in fiction is, of course, Uncle Tom, the hero of Harriet Beecher Stowe's novel, *Uncle Tom's Cabin* (1852). The dramatic power shown in this book is undeniable. More

---

[1] For the body servant in later literature see *The Negro in Southern Literature since the War*, by B. M. Drake (Dissertation, Vanderbilt University, 1898), pp. 21-22.

[2] See in this connection the powerful story by Joel Chandler Harris, *Free Joe and the Rest of the World* (in *Free Joe and Other Georgian Sketches*, 1887). For the freedman in the North, see a paragraph in Robert Y. Hayne's speech in reply to Daniel Webster, January 21 and 25, 1830.

than any other one book it hastened the Civil War and made necessary the emancipation of all slaves. But Uncle Tom is portrayed so plainly for a purpose, the scenes in the book are so skillfully arranged to excite public indignation, that we can hardly call it a great work of art or even a work of art at all. Engel[1] represents justly the literary consensus of opinion when he says: "Uebertrieben in einzelnen, unwahr an allen Enden, unkunstlerisch im Aufban und platt in der Sprache, hat es dennoch auf die Gemuter der Amerikanischen Leser, aber auch der europaischen, jenen tiefen Eindruck hervorgerufen wegen seiner menchenfreundlichen Absicht . . . Heute ist der litterarische Anteil an dem Buche so gut wie erloschen."

Mrs. Howe knew the negro chiefly as she had seen him on the right bank of the Mississippi. Ohio was a free state and the negroes that Mrs. Howe talked with in Cincinnati were those that had fled from Kentucky. Uncle Tom is the type of a good man, a man of sterling piety, subjected to bitter servitude and maltreatment; but there is little about him that is distinctively negro. There is no African background. The language that he speaks is a low grade of highly evangelized English but no more distinctive of the negro than of illiterate whites. Let one compare his

---

[1] *Geschichte der nordamerikanischen Literatur* (Leipzig, 1897), S. 54.

language on any page with that of Uncle Remus and the difference will be at once felt. Opening the Uncle Remus stories at random, I find this sentence,—Uncle Remus is telling what he is going to do to the negro that steals his hogs: "An' I boun'," continued Uncle Remus, driving the corncob stopper a little tighter in his deceitful jug [of whiskey] and gathering up his bag, "an I boun' dat my ole muskit'll go off 'tween me an' dat same nigger yet, an' he'll be at de bad een,' an' dis seetful jug'll 'fuse ter go ter de funer'l."[1] The quaint indirectness of that is more distinctive of the old-time negro speech than anything ever said by Uncle Tom.

If the Tendenzroman is not a suitable theater for the display of negro character, neither is the comic minstrel show. The songs written by Stephen Collins Foster retain still their deserved popularity but they do not portray the negro from within. *Old Black Joe, Old Uncle Ned, My Old Kentucky Home, Old Folks at Home* or *Way Down upon the Suwannee River* are the best known songs ever written by an American. Words, music, and sentiment are welded into perfect unity and harmony. The feeling evoked by these songs is perfectly described by Longfellow, in *The Day is Done:*

---
[1] *That Deceitful Jug* (in *Uncle Remus: his Songs and his Sayings,* p. 218).

> "A feeling of sadness and longing
> That is not akin to pain,
> And resembles sorrow only
> As the mist resembles rain."

Old Folks at Home, says Louis C. Elson,[1] "is the chief American folk-song, and Stephen Collins Foster is as truly the folk-song genius of America as Weber or Silcher have been of Germany." On the contrary, Foster can hardly be called a writer of folk-songs at all. His songs are pure sentimentality; while the old-time negro was religious, musical, humorous, emotional, philosophical, almost everything in fact except sentimental. These songs are not folk-songs, therefore, because the dialect is purely artificial, because neither words nor music originated with the negroes, and because the sentiment they express is alien to the race by whom these songs are supposed to be sung. They are sung, in fact, so far as my observation goes, only by white people, never by negroes, except in a minstrel show.

The man who really discovered the literary material latent in negro character and in negro dialect was Irwin Russell, of Mississippi. The two men best qualified to pass judgment, Joel Chandler Harris and

---

[1] *History of American Music* (1904). See also the sketch of Foster by John L. Cowan in *The Taylor-Trotwood Magazine* (Nashville, Tennessee, December, 1909).

Thomas Nelson Page, have both borne grateful testimony to Russell's genius and to their indebtedness to him. It is pleasant to record also that the first marble bust that the state of Mississippi has placed in her Hall of Fame is that of Irwin Russell.

Russell's greatest poem is *Christmas Night in the Quarters* (1878). In its fidelity to the humble life that it seeks to portray, in the simplicity of its style, the genuineness of its feeling, the distinctness of its pictures, and the sympathy that inspires it, *Christmas Night* belongs in the class with Burns's *Cotter's Saturday Night* and Whittier's *Snow-Bound*. "Burns," said Russell, "is my idol. He seems to me the greatest man that God ever created, beside whom all other poets are utterly insignificant." This poem differs from the works hitherto considered in four important respects: 1. The negro is the central character, the poem being written not to exploit him but to portray him. 2. The dialect, both in its grammar and its rhetoric, is an improvement on everything that had preceded it. 3. The mingling of humor and religion is admirably true to life but had been hitherto unachieved. 4. The explanation of why the possum has no hair on his tail[1] may be considered the beginning of negro folk-lore in American literature.

---
[1] See another explanation in *Uncle Remus: his Songs and his Sayings*, p. 115, and another in *Nights with Uncle Remus*, Introduction, xxx.

It is evident, therefore, that Joel Chandler Harris came at a time when the interest in the negro was at its height. His value as literary material had been realized in part but no satisfactory portrait of him had been drawn. The war, too, with its attendant saturnalia of reconstruction was over, and the negro was trying to fit himself into a new political and industrial regime. It will be seen also that Uncle Remus is a very different character from those by which the negro had hitherto found representation in literature. The character of Uncle Remus is noteworthy not only because it represents both a type and an individual, but because the type is now nearly extinct. Before the war every large plantation or group of plantations had its Uncle Remus; today he lingers here and there in a few villages of the South[1] but is regarded more as a curiosity, a specimen, a relic of the past than as a part of the present.

As portrayed by Harris, Uncle Remus sums up the past and dimly hints the future. The character was modeled after that of an old negro whom Harris had learned to know intimately on the Turner plantation. The Uncle Remus of the stories is eighty years old, but still moves and speaks with the vigor of youth. "He had always exercised authority over his fellow-servants. He had been the captain of the corn-pile,

---

[1] See *The Old-Time Negro*, by Thomas Nelson Page (*Works*, vol. XII, Plantation Edition, Scribner's, N. Y.).

the stoutest at the log-rolling, the swiftest with the hoe, the neatest with the plough, and the plantation hands still looked upon him as their leader."[1] His life has spanned three distinct and widely divergent periods; he has looked out upon three worlds: the South before the war, the South during the war, and the South after the war. He is tenderly cared for by his former owners "Mars John" and "Miss Sally;" he has his own little patch of ground around his cabin; and he is devotedly attached to Miss Sally's "little boy." In spite of their difference in years, the child and the old man have one point in common: they both look out upon the world with eager, wide-eyed interest. Uncle Remus expresses their common point of view in a conversation with Brer Ab. Brer Ab had been telling Uncle Remus of some of the miraculous things seen by a colored woman in a trance: "She say she meet er angel in de road, an' he pinted straight fer de mornin' star, and tell her fer ter prepar'. Hit look mighty cu'us, Brer Remus." "Cum down ter dat, Brer Ab," said Uncle Remus, wiping his spectacles carefully, and readjusting them—"cum down ter dat, an' dey ain't nuffin' dat ain't cu'us."[2]

---

[1] *Nights with Uncle Remus* (1883), p. 400.
[2] *Uncle Remus: his Songs and his Sayings*, p. 212.

Acting on this Aristotelian maxim, Uncle Remus explains to the little boy the mysteries of animal life, especially as they embody themselves in the character of the rabbit and the fox. The humor is entirely unconscious. It is not that of the *Uebermensch*, for the humor of the *Uebermensch* springs from the consciousness of intellectual power, and is, moreover, direct, cynical, self-assertive, masterful. The humor of Uncle Remus represents the underworld of the Underman; it has no reasoned philosophy but springs from the universal desire to correlate the unknown with the known and to explain the most mysterious things by reference to the most obvious. If the rabbit lost his long tail on a certain historic occasion, then all the rabbits born since will have short tails. In fact Uncle Remus's philosophy is perfectly consistent in one thing: all physical characteristics, whether natural or acquired, find their explanation not in past conditions but in past events.

After all, however, the language of Uncle Remus is more interesting than his philosophy. In the picturesqueness of his phrases, in the unexpectedness of his comparisons, in the variety of his figures of speech, in the perfect harmony between the thing said and the way of saying it, the reader finds not only a keen æsthetic delight but even an intellectual satisfaction. It is probable that Uncle Remus's vocabulary would be found, on investigation, to be narrowly limited.

If so, he is a striking evidence of the varied effects that can be produced with but few words, provided these words have been thoroughly assimilated. He leaves the impression not of weakness but of strength, not of contractedness but of freedom. What he says has not only been thought through but seen through and felt through.

It is only after repeated readings that one realizes how completely the character of Uncle Remus is revealed, or rather how completely he is made to reveal himself. There are not many subjects within his range, or beyond it, on which he has not somewhere registered an interesting opinion. If animals are his specialty, he is none the less willing to comment on negroes before and after the war, his favorite dishes, revivals, courtship, Christmas, witches, and religion. These are some of the elemental things about which his thoughts play and through which we come at last to know him and to revere him. Never in American literature has an author succeeded better in harmonizing a typical character with an individual character than has been done in the character of Uncle Remus. He is the first as he is the last adequate portrait of the old-time Southern negro.

But Uncle Remus is interesting not merely in himself but also for the folk-tales of which he is the mouthpiece. These tales mark indeed the beginning of the scientific study of negro folk-lore in America. The author had, however, no ethnological purpose in publishing the Uncle Remus stories and was greatly surprised to learn afterwards that variants of some of his tales had been found among the Indians of North and South America. One story, indeed, has been traced to India and Siam. As to the accuracy with which these stories are reproduced the author speaks as follows:[1] "With respect to the folk-lore series, my purpose has been to preserve the legends themselves in their original simplicity, and to wed them permanently to the quaint dialect—if, indeed, it can be called a dialect—through the medium of which they have become a part of the domestic history of every Southern family; and I have endeavored to give the whole a genuine flavor of the old plantation. Each legend has its variants, but in every instance I have retained that particular version which seemed to me to be the most characteristic, and have given it without embellishment and without exaggeration."

The animals that figure in these stories are, in addition to the fox and the rabbit, the possum, the cow, the terrapin, the wolf, the frog, the bear, the lion, the pig, the deer, the alligator, the snake, the wildcat, the ram, the mink, the weasel, and the dog; among their feathered friends are the buzzard, the guinea-fowl, the hawk, the sparrow, and the goose. Why the

---

[1] *Uncle Remus: his Songs and his Sayings*, introduction, p. 3.

rabbit should be the hero rather than the fox has been differently explained. Harris's own view seems, however, most in accord with the facts: "The story of the rabbit and the fox, as told by the Southern negroes . . . seems to me to be to a certain extent allegorical, albeit such an interpretation may be unreasonable. At least it is a fable thoroughly characteristic of the negro; and it needs no scientific investigation to show why he selects as his hero the weakest and most harmless of all animals, and brings him out victorious in contests with the bear, the wolf, and the fox. It is not virtue that triumphs, but helplessness; it is not malice but mischievousness."

The origin of these tales is still in a measure unsettled, and there is urgent need of more scientific investigation of them. For a while it was thought that the negroes learned these stories from the Indians. It is at least certain that many of the Uncle Remus stories are current among the Indians of North and South America. It is equally certain that more is known of Indian folk-lore than of negro folk-lore. The present status of the question is overwhelmingly in favor of an African origin. The negro slaves, in other words, brought these stories with them from Africa to Brazil and the United States. The Indians in both countries learned them from the negroes.[1]

---

[1] See T. F. Crane's scholarly review of the first volume of the Uncle Remus stories (*Popular Science Monthly*, April, 1881).

A few words now about dialect in general and the dialect of the Uncle Remus stories in particular. A great deal of investigation still needs to be done before American dialects can be accurately discriminated, but a few points at least may be considered as settled. The first impetus to the employment of dialect in American literature was given by James Russell Lowell in the first and second series of *The Biglow Papers* (1848, 1866). The dialect of *The Biglow Papers*, though confined to New England, contains only a few words and phrases that would not be instantly understood in the West and South. Though Lowell's effort was entirely successful, his example did not bear fruit until after 1870. The early masters of the short story, Irving, Poe, and Hawthorne, disdained the use of dialect, as did Longfellow and Whittier in their abolition poems. Had Whittier been familiar with the negro dialect, his anti-slavery poems would have gained in force and effectiveness. Such a poem as *The Farewell of a Virginia Slave Mother to her Daughters* (1838) is rendered simply ludicrous by the refrain "Woe is me, my stolen daughters." So classic a phrase as "Woe is me" might well have befitted the lips of one of Milton's warriors but was as impossible to a negro slave as to his white owner.

In 1870 Lowell published his scholarly Introduction to *The Biglow Papers*. At the same time Bret Harte gave new force to Lowell's views by the skill with which he employed the mixed dialects of California in his stories of the forty-niners. The year 1870, therefore, which witnessed, as we have seen, a new development of the short story, witnessed also a new development of dialect. Bret Harte, writing in 1899,[1] mentions as the leading American short story writers, then living, Joel Chandler Harris, George W. Cable, Mark Twain in *Huckleberry Finn*, "Charles Egbert Craddock" (Miss Murfree), and Mary E. Wilkins (now Mrs. Freeman). These names, together with that of Bret Harte himself, show that excellence in dialect and excellence in the short story have been almost synonymous in American literature since 1870.

What is needed now above all in the study of the American short story is a work on dialect in American literature since 1870. The varieties are not many, and the resemblances are far greater than the differences. The negro dialect diverges of course more from standard English than does any other recognized American dialect; but it is easier than the others because of its limited vocabulary and because the law of analogy (die Wirkung der Analogie), as in the case of children, has eliminated almost all exceptions. Wherever negro English has developed without the admixture of foreign languages it has been dominated

---

[1] "The Rise of the Short Story," *The Cornhill Magazine*, July.

in sound, syntax, and Formenlehre by the principle of analogy.[1]

Of the negro dialect in general, as spoken in America, there are four varieties. 1. The dialect of Virginia, especially of Eastern or Tidewater Virginia. 2. The dialect of the Sea Islands of the South Atlantic States, known as the Gullah (or Gulla) dialect. 3. The dialect spoken by the Creole negroes of Louisiana. 4. The dialect not included in the three preceding groups, that is, the dialect spoken by the negroes in the inland sections of the South and Southwest.

The negro dialect of Virginia is best represented in the works of Thomas Nelson Page. The *a* in this dialect is very broad, and there is a vanishing y-sound heard after c (k z) and g (g z) when broad *a* follows them: *larst* (*last*), *pahsture* (*pasture*), *pahf* (*path*), *cyarn'* (*can't*), *kyars* (*cars*), *gyardin* (*garden*).

The Gullah (Gulla)[2] dialect is the dialect of the rice plantations of South Carolina and Georgia, as the Uncle Remus dialect is that of the cotton and tobacco plantations further inland. It varies widely from standard English and in its most primitive state is "merely a confused and untranslatable mixture of

---

[1] For a discussion of this principle, see Paul's *Prinzipien der Sprachgeschichte*, (4th edition, 1909, Halle), chapter V.

[2] The name is doubtless derived from Angola, as many of the rice-field negroes of South Carolina and Georgia are known to have come originally from the east coast of Africa.

English and African words." Its use by Poe in the *Gold-Bug*, by Simms in *The Yemassee*,[1] and by Harris in *Nights with Uncle Remus* has already been touched upon. The best representation of Gullah in recent fiction is in *The Treasure of Peyre Gaillard* (1906), by John Bennet.[2]

The dialect spoken by the Creole negroes of Southern Louisiana is, of course, not English but French. "It is quite interesting," says Alcee Fortier,[3] "to note how the ignorant and simple Africans have formed an idiom entirely by the sound, and we can understand, by studying the transformation of the French into the Creole dialect, the process by which Latin, spoken by the uncivilized Gauls, became our own French." This dialect can best be studied in the works of George W. Cable. It is employed sparingly, however, because to one not familiar with French it is as unintelligible as Gullah is to one unfamiliar with English.

The dialect spoken by the great majority of the uneducated negroes of the United States is that of the Uncle Remus stories. There have been changes in vocabulary and a decline also in vigor and picturesqueness of expression, due of course, to the influence

---
[1] It is found also in *Woodcraft*, or *The Sword and the Distaff*, (1854), by Simms.
[2] See the *Library of Southern Literature*, vol. 1, pp. 323-328. Bennet is better known as the author of *Master Skylark* (1897), a story of Elizabethan times.
[3] *Louisiana Studies* (New Orleans, 1894), p. 134.

of negro schools and to the passing of the old plantation life. But the language used by Uncle Remus still embodies the characteristic qualities of negro speech as heard especially in the country districts of the South.

The most distinctive thing about the Uncle Remus dialect, apart from phonology, is found in the *Formenlehre* of the verb. Uncle Remus does not say, for example, *I make, you make, he makes,* but *I makes, you makes, we makes, you makes, dey makes.* Negro dialect is, in other words, an ear language, and the law of analogy has unfettered operation. The negro, hearing the third person singular with its *s*-ending more frequently than any other form of the present indicative, makes it the norm and uses it in all persons and in both numbers. The same is true of the verb *to be*, though the plural has not been entirely eliminated.

The past tense of weak verbs sometimes adds *ed* (*t*) but more frequently presents the simple stem: *I hear* (*heard*), *I talk* (*talked*), *I make* (*made*). Since the *s*-ending is the sign of the present tense, the simple stem without the *s*-ending can be used without confusion as the sign of the past tense. Among the weak verbs that form their past tense without or with *ed* (*t*) may be mentioned: *holler* (=*hollered*), *drap* (=*drapt*), *kyar* (=*kyard*), *stay* (=*stayed*), *draw* (=*draw'd*). In the case of strong verbs there is usually a vowel change, and the past participle is usually the same as the preterit indicative: *I sot* (*set* or *sat*), *I hilt* (*held*), *I tuck* (*took*), *I cotch* (*caught*), *I shuck* (*shook*), *I gun* or *gin* (*gave*), *I gun* or *begun* (*began*), *I done* (*did*), *I brung* (*brought*), *I seed* (*saw*). The past tense of *to be* is *wuz* (*was*) for all persons and both numbers.

The future tense is formed sometimes with *will* (*I'll, you'll,* etc.) but more commonly with *gwineter* (*going to*).

The three tenses may therefore be summarized as follows:

PRESENT[1]

I	wants,	takes,	sees	:	I is, am, I'm
You	"	"	"	:	You is, youer
He, she, hit,	"	"	"	:	He, she, hit is ('s)
We	"	"	"	:	We is, we's, we er
You	"	"	"	:	You is, youer
Dey	"	"	"	:	Dey is, dey's, dey er

PAST

I	want,	tuck,	seed	:	I wuz, I'uz
You	"	"	"	:	You wuz, you'uz

---

[1] In a few cases the *s* is dropped: *I hear, fo' I kick, I speck, you look, hit look like, w'en de cashun come.*

He, she, hit, want, tuck, seed : He, she, hit wuz ('uz)
We   "   "   "   : We wuz, we 'uz
You   "   "   "   : You wuz, you 'uz
Dey   "   "   "   : Dey wuz, dey 'uz

FUTURE

I'm gwineter take, see, be
You gwineter take, see, be
We gwineter, We's gwineter take, see, be
You gwineter, You's gwineter take, see, be
Dey gwineter, Dey's gwineter.

BIBLIOGRAPHY

Bibliographies may be found in the *Monthly Bulletin,* Carnegie Library, Atlanta, Georgia, May-June, 1907, and in the *Library* of *Southern Literature* (Atlanta, 1909), vol. V, pp. 2118-2120. Shortly after Harris's death brief appraisals of his work were published in:

The Nation, July 9, 1908.
Harper's Weekly, July 11, 1908.
The Independent, July 23, 1908.
Current Literature, August, 1908.
The Bookman, August, 1908.
Review of Reviews, August, 1908.
South Atlantic Quarterly (Durham, N. C.) October, 1908.

Century Magazine, April, 1909.
See also Schönbach's Gesammelte Aufsätze (Graz, 1900), S. 432.

NEGRO FOLK-LORE

African Native Literature, by S. W. Koelle (London, 1854).

Reynard the Fox in South Africa, by W. H. G. Bleek (London, 1864).

The Myths of the New World, by D. G. Brinton (N. Y., 1868).

Amazonian Tortoise Myths, by C. F. Hartt (1875).

Folk-Lore of the Southern Negroes, William Owens (*Lippincott's Magazine*, December, 1877).

Brazil and the Amazons, by H. H. Smith (1880).

Uncle Remus: his Songs and his Sayings, introduction by Joel Chandler Harris (1880).

Plantation Folk-Lore, by T. F. Crane (*Popular Science Monthly*, April, 1881).

Kaffir Folk-Lore, by George McCall Theal (London, 1882).

Nights with Uncle Remus, introduction by Joel Chandler Harris, (1883).

Bits of Louisiana Folk-Lore, by Alcee Fortier (*Transactions and Proceedings of the Modern Language Association of America*, vol. III, 1887).

Negro Myths from the Georgia Coast, by C. C. Jones (1888).

Folk-Lore, by B. M. Drake (*The Negro in Southern Literature since the War,* Dissertation, Vanderbilt University, 1898).

Religious Folk Songs of the Negro, as sung on the Plantations, by Robert R. Moton (1909, first edition 1874). This is the standard collection of genuine negro songs.

Voodoo Tales as Told Among the Negroes of the Southwest, by Mary O. Owen (N. Y., 1893), with introduction by Charles Godfrey Leland.

Negro Dialect

Slave Songs of the United States, by W. F. Allen, C. P. Ware, and L. McK. Garrison (1867).

The Creole Patois of Louisiana, by James A. Harrison (*American Journal of Philology,* III, 1882). Contains remarks also on the Creole negro dialect.

Negro English, by James A. Harrison (*Anglia, VII,* 1884).

Southern Dialect, by Harry Stillwell Edwards (*Century Magazine, L*).

The Creole Dialect, by Alcee Fortier (*Louisiana Studies,* New Orleans, 1894).

Uncle Remus in Phonetic Spelling, by J. P. Fruit (*Dialect Notes*, vol. I, 1896).

Negro Dialect, by B. M. Drake (*The Negro in Southern Literature since the War*, Dissertation, Vanderbilt University, 1898).

On the negroes' contributions to literature, see *The Negro in Literature and Art*, by Benjamin Griffith Brawley (Atlanta, Ga., 1910).

O. HENRY—THE MAN AND HIS WORK [1]

O. HENRY'S last words spoken with a smile, were, "I don't want to go home in the dark." Could he return to us he would find that he did not go home in the dark, but that an increasing radiance shines about his name and fame. He is read today not only in English but also in French, Spanish, German, Swedish, Dano-Norwegian and Japanese. "I'm not a critic," a woman said to me in Brooklyn recently, "and know nothing about the technique of the short story. But I do know that, whenever I feel low-spirited, O. Henry is my best restorative." She is typical, I think, of O. Henry's large and increasing clientele of readers. They not only read him but come more and more under the spell of his genial and companionable nature. The entertainer has become both friend and comrade. The best loved author in English literature is probably Oliver Goldsmith or Charles Lamb. In American literature the choice would lie, I think, between Washington Irving and O. Henry.

It is too soon to speak with any claim to finality about O. Henry's place in American literature, but certain phases of his work are beginning already to

---

[1] Reprinted from *The Mentor*, February, 1923. Dr. Smith was a life-long friend of O. Henry and author of his authorized biography.

loom up as salient and distinctive. He is, for example, the only writer in English or American literature who won his place solely by the writing of short stories. Irving soon passed from the story to history and biography; Hawthorne "found himself famous" only after he began his wider career as a novelist; Poe was a critic, short-story writer, and poet; Bret Harte is our greatest parodist, but it is impossible—thinks his latest biographer—to say whether he will make "his appeal to posterity mainly as a poet or prose writer;" Henry James attained his most characteristic expression in the novel; Stevenson and Kipling would be secure in their immortality if they had never written a short story. In singleness of impression, therefore, as well as in bulk, O. Henry's two hundred and fifty short stories represent the most significant effort yet made by an English-speaking writer to win and hold a place in letters not by that loose thing known as the story that is short, but by that artistic triumph known as the "short story."

O. Henry is also the only short-story writer known to us whose workshop contained no rejected manuscripts. Some of his stories were widely traveled, he tells us, but they all landed at last. "My first story," he said, "was paid for, but I never saw it in print." This was *The Miracle of Lava Cañon*, which was accepted by the McClure Company on December 2, 1897, and marked for "publication September 18,

1898." From this date to the appearance of his last story, *Let Me Feel Your Pulse*, published shortly after his death, *every story* submitted to a publisher was sooner or later accepted. This unique record is a testimonial to the faith that O. Henry kept with his art. "Write to please yourself," he once gave as the only rule, and from this high standard he never swerved. The story must be as good as he could make it before he was willing for the public to see it.

It will help us to appraise O. Henry's art if we remember that he did not find himself in the short story at once. Even after he had won national recognition by the publication of "The Four Million" in 1906, he felt the call of other types and of other talents. In the last conversation that I had with him, in New York, in February, 1908, he talked glowingly of a drama upon which he was engaged, and spoke weariedly about the demands made upon him by the publishers to whom he had promised short stories before they were completely written. "Sometimes there will come a telephone message about two o'clock in the morning," he remarked, "saying, 'We must have the rest of that story today.' I ask them to read me the last paragraph of the first instalment so that I can know just where to start." I told him that I didn't believe a word of this, that his stories were so notable for their unity as to prove a continuousness in the creative process, even if the story were not all written at once. But he continued to proclaim the superiority of the drama. The drama that he had in mind, however, was not a new creation. It was a reshaping of his short story "The World and the Door," in which he believed that he had hit upon a great truth, viz., "that every human soul has this tendency toward respectability, that it is greater than love;" nobody, thought O. Henry should be classed as permanently down and out. In boyhood days it was not the drama or the short story that drew him; it was the cartoonist's art. To our way of thinking, no such youthful genius in pen or pencil sketch had yet appeared. Later on, he tried his hand as editor of *The Rolling Stone* in Austin, Texas, and as reporter on *The Houston Post*. After his establishment in New York he felt the lure not only of the drama but also of poetry, the musical comedy, and the autobiographical novel. But all these diversions, though they lessened the number of short stories that he might have written, contributed indirectly to the excellence of those that he did write; they flowed *from* his art at first, but returned later in deepened volume *to* it. Nothing helps a man more to do what he can do than to know what he can't do.

The first impression that the reader of O. Henry gets is one of originality. O. Henry was a voice, not an echo. He has been compared with many writers,

American and foreign, but no one has called him an imitator of any one else. The O. Henry touch is altogether distinctive in narrative art. He had read much, thought much, and suffered much before he became famous. But every discipline had developed him centrally rather than marginally. If you were thrown with him often you would have observed in him a great equality rather than a steep superiority. I have never known a nature so widely receptive as his, but at the same time so eagerly but quietly reactive. His reactions, however, were not those of criticism or rejection. They partook more of the nature of an instinctive human interest, of a wide and liberal understanding, of a keen but sympathetic determination to see life just as you saw it. The critical judgment must wait. Talk with him five minutes and he could reproduce you to a button in a pencil sketch, and probably reveal some central trait in you unknown even to yourself. There would certainly be something amusing about you, though no one else may ever have discovered it before.

His originality, therefore, is not the originality of novel things but of old things probed a little more deeply. He took old themes—love, habit, the voiceless part of our population, the humor and pathos of daily life, the West versus the East, the South versus the North, the romance and unexpectedness of the commonplace, the things that you and I have in common—and gave them a new meaning, a new interest, a new appeal. Even his literary allusions are of the old-fashioned sort. Though he was saturated with magazine literature and newspaper happenings, the books that had left the deepest impress upon him were the Bible, Shakespeare, Tennyson, and the Arabian Nights. To the Bible he makes his largest number of references, sixty-three; to Shakespeare, thirty-four; to Tennyson, twenty-one; to the Arabian Nights, fourteen. These were familiar to him from childhood, and his use of them indicates anew the quality of his originality. Instead of exploiting the new, he reinterpreted the old.

Much has been written about O. Henry's humor as shown in his calculated misquotations, his inverted phrasing, his verbal coruscations. But O. Henry's humor is only incidentally a thing of words and phrases. You may omit these and O. Henry would still be a great humorist. Had these been essential, his stories could never have survived translation, for translation shears away remorselessly all that is merely verbal. No, O. Henry's characters are not humorous because they say funny things. They *say funny things because they are humorous.* O. Henry's humor has been acclaimed by a world of grateful readers because, like the humor of Shakespeare and Molière and Cervantes, it rises naturally and spontaneously from the situations in which his characters are placed. The situations become themselves creative; they belong to the elemental nature of comedy. They are matrix rather than copy, and the humor is born rather than made. Review the situations in *The Handbook of Hymen*, *A Cosmopolite in a Cafè*, *The Brief Début of Tildy*, *A Lickpenny Lover*, *Two Renegades*, *The Gift of the Magi*, *The Cop and the Anthem*, *Makes the Whole World Kin*, *The Lady Higher Up*, *The Pendulum*, *The Making of a New Yorker*. In each of these the stage is set by a master. There is subtle thought, even profound thought, not so much in the working out of the plots as in the selection and fore-staging of such humorous situations as make the plots work themselves out. Humor is released rather than manufactured. It plays hide-and-seek with pathos in many of these stories, and not infrequently both humor and pathos come before the footlights hand in hand to receive the plaudits of an audience that finds it hard to say which is which.

A special distinction of O. Henry's humor is that it is not harsh, or cynical, or derisive. It is humane because it is fundamentally human. It is associative rather than separative in its effect. As soon as you read one of his stories you want to read it aloud to others. But you do not have to pick your audience for fear that feelings will be hurt. Rich or poor, educated or illiterate, employer or employee, black or white, man or woman—all will find their common heritage of humanity reached and enriched. Much of the stage humor of today, certainly that of the school of Wilde and Shaw, derives most of its sparkle from what has been called "the neat reversal of middle-class conceptions." There is no such reversal in O. Henry. Instead of pitting class against class, he reveals class to class and section to section. He seems to say: "You think the other fellow is funny. Well, you are just as funny as he is."

With his originality and humor must be considered his Americanism. He never visited England or the Continent. But he knew his own country; and his journeyings in Central America, South America, and Mexico gave him just the angle of contrast that was needed to enable him to run the boundary line sharply between what was American and what was not. If we omit the stories of New York and Texas, which include one hundred and seventy titles, there are left twenty additional states represented by O. Henry's backgrounds. If he had not visited all of these and studied their regional differentials at first hand, he had at least heard intimately about them. He knew them accurately enough to make both plot and characters fit naturally and revealingly into each setting that he chose.

But Americanism is not a matter of geography. It is a spirit, a mood, a temperament, an attitude toward men and things, a way of looking at life, of expressing life, and of achieving life. Foreigners detect it more readily than we do. Thus Hugh Walpole, writing in the *London Daily Mail*, declares that American literature has at last become "independent"; and he hails O. Henry as "the true father of this new American literature."

It is impossible to corral Americanism in the confines of a scientific definition, but one element of O. Henry's Americanism emerges in a report that came from the battlefields of France. "As a trench companion," so ran a soldier's comment, "O. Henry cannot be surpassed. He is brief, he is witty, he is deliciously human. Without meaning to, apparently, he teaches a philosophy of cheerful acceptance of 'The Things That Are To Be.'" Add to this his instinctive aversion to indecency in every form; recall, too, his exacting idealism which made him say almost with his latest breath, "I want to get at something bigger. What I have done is child's play to what I can do, to what I know it is in me to do"—and you have the American, the artist, and the man in one.

A short poem, "The Crucible," was found on O. Henry's desk after his death. Nothing that he ever wrote is more truly or tenderly autobiographic.

"Hard ye may be in the tumult,
Red to your battle hilts,
Blow give for blow in the foray,
Cunningly ride in the tilts;
But when the roaring is ended,
Tenderly, unbeguiled,
Turn to a woman a woman's
Heart, and a child's to a child.

"Test of the man if his worth be
In accord with the ultimate plan,
That he be not to his marring,
Always and utterly man;
That he bring out of the tumult,
Fitter and undefiled,
To a woman the heart of a woman,
To children the heart of a child.

"Good when the bugles are ranting
It is to be iron and fire;
Good to be oak in the foray,
Ice to a guilty desire.
But when the battle is over
(Marvel and wonder the while)
Give to a woman a woman's
Heart, and a child's to a child."

MATTHEW FONTAINE MAURY [1]

THERE is a peculiar propriety in the erection of a memorial to Matthew Fontaine Maury in Goshen Pass. Of all the pleasant places of earth, it was this place that swam last before his dying vision. It was from the beauty of this spot, treasured in his memory, that he passed into the realm of changeless and unfading beauty. It was the flowers that grow here, between Laurel Run and Anchor Rock, that he wished placed upon his coffin body as the last and only tribute of affection:

> "Wait till the laurel bursts its buds,
>   And creeping ivy flings its graces
> About the lichen'd rocks, and floods
>   Of sunshine fill the shady places.
>
> "Then, when the sky, the air, the grass,
>   Sweet Nature all, is glad and tender,
> Then bear me through the Goshen Pass
>   Amid its flush of May-day splendor."

Fifty years ago they bore him lovingly through this Pass and heaped the flowers upon him. Today we

---

[1] An address delivered at the unveiling of a tablet to Maury in Goshen Pass, Virginia, June 9, 1923. The substance of this address was also delivered before the University of Virginia Summer School, August 10, 1923, and at the unveiling of the Maury portrait presented to the U. S. Naval Academy by the United Daughters of the Confederacy, November 20, 1923.

MATTHEW FONTAINE MAURY 169

wish him to abide here. As he did not forget Goshen Pass, so Goshen Pass has not forgotten him. This tablet is the pledge of a mutual love and constancy that will know neither variableness nor the shadow of turning.

This is neither the time nor the place for a biography of Matthew Fontaine Maury. I shall attempt only to say what seems to me the distinctive contribution that Maury has made to science and to civilization. That he has made such a contribution is evident. Why, for example, should a distinguished writer who had never heard of Maury till he visited Virginia add after a few days of investigation: "Yet there is no one living in the United States, or in any civilized country, whose daily life is not affected through the scientific researches and attainments of this man?" Why is it that the United States Government publishes through the Hydrographic Office in Washington four great charts every month and puts at the top of each: "Founded upon the researches made and the data collected by Lieut. M. F. Maury, U. S. Navy?" This is a recognition paid to no other naval officer and these charts perform a service and have for three quarters of a century performed a service without parallel among government publications. Something that Maury thought and something that he did have plainly become the heritage of the ages and this heritage has grown rather than diminished with every passing year.

The great thought on which Maury was to build came to him at the age of twenty-five. It was in the year 1831. This thought was that the sea, if investigated, would be found to have its laws as constant, as uniform, as invariable as those of the land. Nature to Maury was one and indivisible. She was as sovereign over the three-fourths of the world which was fluid as over the one-fourth which was solid. The waves, the winds, the storms, the currents, the depths, and the temperatures of the sea were believed by Maury to constitute a system, a complex of cause and effect, constant in its regularity, perfect in its orderliness, and so mathematically interrelated that the mind of man could by patient investigation understand its phenomena and even forecast its processes. It was more than a theory with Maury. It was a faith, the kind of antecedent faith that had led Columbus, Galileo, Harvey, and Newton to their respective goals.

Tennyson makes Columbus say from his chains,

> "The golden guess
> Is morning-star to the full round of truth.
> No guess-work! I was certain of my goal."

So was Maury. Eleven years were to pass before he could put his faith to the test of actual proof. But the very intensity of his belief, the vividness with which he saw and felt the integrity of nature and the inviolability of her laws on sea as well as on land, was to him in the nature of a demonstration.

It was easy for men to believe, even before proof came, that the quiet land was the abode of natural law. Its regularly recurrent seasons, its testimonials of evenly laid strata, its ancient forms of animal and vegetable life, its visible adaptations of form and function to climate and soil, all spoke of an orderly development which by investigation man could in part understand and control. But the sea was different. It was the very symbol of caprice and lawlessness; it suggested the unknown and the unknowable. If it had its laws, they seemed beyond the reach of rational explanation. When Byron wrote, a few years before,

> "Roll on, thou deep and dark blue Ocean, roll!
> Ten thousand fleets sweep over thee in vain;
> Man marks the earth with ruin, his control
> Stops with the shore."

he expressed the prevailing attitude. Fleets did sweep over the ocean in vain so far as collective research or helpful data were concerned. Man's control did stop with the shore so far as control was dependent on the understanding of winds and currents and a compliance with their inexorable demands. When Baron von Humboldt, twenty-five years later, wrote his monumental *Cosmos*, conditions were practically the same. Though his book was considered the last word on science up to the year 1844, his scant treatment of "oceanic discoveries" is but added proof that Maury was an unheralded pioneer. Had Humboldt deferred his discussion of the ocean until 1855, Maury's name instead of being unmentioned would have led the list of marine discoverers; for in 1855, Humboldt had recognized in Maury the master scientist of the sea and had acclaimed him as a world benefactor.

Whether Maury at the age of twenty-five had thought of any definite means of proving his faith in the sea, I do not know. I think that he had. In a letter written to his brother in 1833, Maury speaks of resigning from the Navy, adding, however, "I have too many notions." These notions held him, and they seem to imply not merely a new view about the sea but some hoped for plan of carrying this view into effect. In the meanwhile, though only "a passed midshipman," he was growing in knowledge, range, and power. In 1836, he published his *Navigation*, a book that almost immediately displaced all rivals and remained till recent years the authoritative text on that subject. It is interesting to recall that Edgar Allan Poe was one of the first to proclaim the merits of the new book and to welcome in it the new spirit of research that was beginning to manifest itself in the American navy. In 1839, Maury's leg was broken in a stage-coach accident and he limped the rest of his life. He at once turned all the more resolutely to study and investigation and began to publish in the *Southern Literary Messenger* a series of articles called "Scraps from the Lucky Bag of Harry Bluff, U. S. N." Nobody knew who the author was but the criticisms of the navy, though severe, were so wisely constructive that naval officers not only welcomed them but set about embodying them in a new and better naval organization. There can be little doubt that the Naval Academy, founded at Annapolis in 1845, is the product of the suggestions made by Maury in these articles.

In 1842 the great opportunity came. Maury was sent to Washington and placed in charge of the Depot of Charts and Instruments which he quickly converted into the National Observatory and Hydrographical Department of the United States. The man, the hour, and the task had met; and Maury was about to become the best known and most widely honored American living. He was to make our Hydrographic Office the observed of all observatories, and he was to prove to all scientists and to the mariners of all seas that the ocean is as law abiding as the land.

The method that he pursued was almost as fruitful as the results obtained. It was the method of cooperation. He had blank forms, abstract logs, as he called them, prepared and sent out to all ships that would use them. These called for a sort of recorded diary of temperatures, air pressures, depths, winds, and currents over every surface of every sea that was traversed. The sea was asked to grant a continuous interview and thus to have its autobiography written. This it did willingly, never having been persuasively asked before. As soon as a thousand coworkers had submitted their chapters, Maury was ready with his pilot charts and sailing directions, and these with a few changes but with Maury's name at the top are still piloting the ships of all the seas.

The effect on navigation was immediate and dramatic. As it was on the *Falmouth,* sailing from New York to Rio de Janeiro, that Maury had first thought about uniform winds and currents, he determined to make the first test of his charts on this route. The voyage was cut in half. In 1848, gold was discovered in California and our great clipper ships began to race with their freights from New York around Cape Horn to San Francisco. The average voyage was 183 days; it was reduced at once by Maury to 135 days. One American clipper, the *Flying Cloud,* keeping close to Maury's sea lanes, accomplished the trip in 89 days, making 374 miles in one day. No Atlantic steamer of the time had made such a day's run. So favoring were the winds along Maury's routes that many an American clipper covered the 16,000 miles from New York to San Francisco without having to reef her topsails more than twice. Gold was discovered a little later in Australia and the average trip from England to the Australian mines was reduced from 124 days to 97 days. The annual saving to the United States alone on freight to and from South America, China, and the East Indies was estimated at 5 million dollars. Maury found that zigzag routes had been followed from time immemorial on the trip from New York to Cape Horn and that the Atlantic was crossed nearly three times needlessly on each voyage. Sailors had heard of terrible currents if they sailed straight, currents which Maury found to be mythical but the fear of which had lengthened the voyages and multiplied the disasters of ships for more than two hundred years. It is easy to estimate the saving of time and money that Maury effected; it is impossible to estimate the number of lives saved or the number of shipwrecks avoided.

But Maury's pinnacle moment was yet to come. His system of sea lanes had been utilized chiefly by American ships, his co-workers also being chiefly Americans. Wonders had been accomplished, it is true. Rivalry at sea had been stimulated; new instruments of measurement had been devised and old ones improved; Americanism had been quickened; a new pride in our naval prowess had been aroused;

and the whole nation had thrilled time and again when the news had come that an American clipper, following Maury's sea paths, had shown her heels to a British steamer, burdened with the coal that she had to carry on the long voyage to Australia. But Maury wanted all nations to coöperate with the United States Observatory and all ships and shipping to be correspondingly benefited.

An international conference was therefore called to meet in Brussels in August, 1853, a memorable date not only for navigation but for international good will and coöperation. It was the first League of Nations. Belgium, Holland, Denmark, Norway, Sweden, Russia, France, Portugal, Great Britain, and the United States attended. Maury was at once nominated for president, but declined the honor in favor of the great Belgian scientist, Quetelet. The conference lasted sixteen days. At its close Maury's meteorological charts had been unanimously adopted and nineteen-twentieths of the shipping of the world had come within the compass of his vast and beneficent design. When the count was made fifty years later it was found that Dutch seamen had turned in $3\frac{1}{2}$ million of the prescribed log books accurately filled out, American seamen $5\frac{1}{2}$ million, British seamen 7 million, and German seamen more than $10\frac{1}{2}$ million. Maury, however, did not wait for these. One year after the great Conference had met, he was enabled from the data received to publish the first depth-map of the North Atlantic and to point out the pathway for the first cable. In 1855 he published his *Physical Geography of the Sea* and inaugurated a new science. It was the first book to embrace the entire sea as its theme and thus to bring three-fourths of the world into the domain of recognized and intelligible principle. If some of its conclusions have been overthrown, as of course they have, let it be remembered that they were overthrown by a method of continuous coöperation which Maury originated and by the testimony of log books which he had drawn up. The trans-Atlantic sea routes, however, which Maury had already charted, have been changed in only one detail since his death. After the wreck of the *Titanic* in 1912, the great liners agreed to dip a little further south to avoid the icebergs. This was not a modification of sea lane; it was a modification only in the time of changing from Maury's more northern to his more southern route.

But the Brussels Conference was more than a scientific triumph. It meant a new era in history. Never before had the great nations of the world come together to plan for the common welfare and to exclude no nation from their counsels. It was agreed that if war came, Maury's log books should in no case be destroyed. Even if the ship were sunk in battle, the nations pledged themselves to rescue the log books and to transmit them to their destination. The data must not be lost. The observations of each must be harvested for the good of all. The past and the present must extend a helping hand to the future. Maury felt keenly the greatness of the moment and sought to turn the consideration of the Conference from himself to the vast moral import of what they were witnessing. When Quetelet at the first meeting thanked Maury in behalf of all the delegates for his services to navigation, Maury replied:

"I am extremely grateful for the sympathy you have expressed and the praise you have been pleased to bestow on my humble efforts. On my part, I beg to thank you for the kind assistance that you have afforded me. Allow me to add, that we are taking part in a proceeding to which we should vainly seek for a parallel in history. Heretofore, when naval officers of different nations met in such numbers, it was to deliberate at the cannons' mouths upon the most efficacious means of destroying the human species. Today, on the contrary, we see assembled the delegates of almost every maritime nation, for the noble purpose of serving humanity by seeking to render navigation more and more secure. I think, gentlemen, we may congratulate ourselves with pride upon the opening of this new era."

One other contribution to the new era Maury was yet to make, but a strange and tragic history was to release him for his new task. He had thought much and written much about the benefits that would accrue to the farmer if weather conditions could be anticipated on land as well as they had been anticipated on the sea. In the concluding remarks that he made in Brussels he expressed the hope that the time would soon come when a general system of observations would be established embracing both land and sea. In 1858 he wrote in one of his "Sailing Directions to Accompany the Wind and Current Charts":

"As much as we have accomplished at sea more yet can be accomplished through the magnetic telegraph on land. With a properly devised system of meteorological observations to be made at certain stations wherever the telegraph spreads its meshes, and to be reported daily by telegrams to a properly organized office, the shipping in the harbors of our seaport towns, the husbandman in the field, and the traveler on the road may all be warned of every extensive storm that visits our shores and while yet it is a great way off."

But there seemed little likelihood that Maury would ever have the opportunity to lead a crusade for a great Weather Bureau on land, though no one was so well fitted for it as he. Every moment of his time was occupied at the Naval Observatory. He had no thought of resigning. He was devoted to his tasks and problems. He was the recognized authority on marine meteorology in all lands. Honors such as no other American had ever received had come to him and were continuing to come to him from foreign governments. But all this was changed in the twinkling of an eye. War came, Maury resigned his position, was sent by the Confederate Government on a diplomatic mission to England, and did not see his native land again until 1868. In that year the University of Cambridge bestowed upon him and upon Tennyson the degree of LL.D. In the same year he declined the directorship of the French Imperial Observatory and accepted the call to the chair of physics in the Virginia Military Institute at Lexington.

Now began the last chapter in Maury's life. The thought of helping the farmers, especially the cotton planters, by the establishment of a more effective Weather Bureau in Washington, inspired him with a zeal and enthusiasm that knew no bounds. He traveled and lectured in every section of the United States. The international mind had always been his and in a short time England and Russia were sending him resolutions of thanks for the stimulation of agriculture which his far-flung addresses had inspired. The chair of physics at the Virginia Military Institute had become the most potent platform in the

United States for the propagation of the new movement.

But he had overtaxed his strength. Returning from a lecture in St. Louis he knew that his career was near its close. He must have known also that the victory had been won, that his sea charts had set the standard for the land charts, and that the task of interpreting nature in terms of help rather than of hindrance for mankind had been permanently advanced by his efforts. The end came quietly on February 1, 1873. "Do I drag my anchors?" he asked with a smile. "Yes," said his son. "All is well," he replied.

We dedicate this tablet to one who, though dead, yet lives and leads. We dedicate it to the founder of a new science, to the pilot of every ship that sails, to the herald of the new era of international cooperation. Matthew Fontaine Maury summed the past and projected the future. Over land and sea his spirit broods in abiding benediction.

BIBLIOGRAPHY OF C. ALPHONSO SMITH

BIBLIOGRAPHY OF C. ALPHONSO SMITH

Some Literary Aspects of the Book of Judges. Presbyterian Quarterly, Richmond, Va., October, 1892.

Poetry in Everyday Life. Davidson Monthly, Davidson, N. C., February-March, 1892.

The Order of Words in Anglo-Saxon Prose. (Johns Hopkins Doctorial Dissertation.) Publications of the Modern Language Association of America (New Series), I, 1893.

Repetition and Parallelism in English Verse. University Publishing Co., New York, 1894.

English Literature in the Public Schools. Proceedings of the Eighth Annual Convention of Parish Superintendents (Louisiana), May, 1894.

Note on the Dramatic Import of the Falling Sickness in Shakespeare's Julius Caesar. Poet-Lore, Boston, VI, 1894.

Note on Skeat's Omission of 'Swete' in Legend of Good Women, line 1338. Mod. Lang. Notes, IX, 1894.

Knowing and Teaching. Proceedings of the Third Annual Convention of the Louisiana State Teachers' Association, December, 1895.

A Note on the Punctuation of Lycidas. Mod. Lang. Notes, XI, 1896.

Shakespeare's Present Indicative s-Endings with Plural Subjects. Publications of the Modern Language Association of America, IV, 1896.

An Old English Grammar and Exercise Book. Allyn and Bacon, Boston, 1896.

Than Whom and Its Congeners. Mod. Lang. Notes, XII, 1898.

The Possibilities of the South in Literature. Sewanee Review, July, 1898.

Van Noppen's Translation of Vondel's Lucifer. Mod. Lang. Notes, XIV, 1899.

The Work of the Modern Language Association of America. Publications of the Modern Language Association of America, VII, 1899.

English in the Secondary School. Proceedings of the Memphis Meeting of the Southern Educational Association, December, 1899.

Jottings from London. Davidson College Magazine, November, 1900.

Interpretative Syntax. Publications of the Modern Language Association of America, VIII, 1900.

Sweet's New English Grammar, Part II, Syntax. Journal of Germanic Philology, III, 1900.

Sidney Lee's Shakespeare's Life and Work. Mod. Lang. Notes, XVI, 1901.

Paris after the Exposition. Charlotte Observer, N. C., January 13, 1901.

Meeting of the German Shakespeare Society. Nation, New York, May 23, 1901.

An Edition of Macaulay's Essays on Milton and Addison. B. F. Johnson Publishing Co., Richmond, Va., 1901.

A Note on the Concord of Collectives and Indefinites. Anglia, XI, 1901.

The Chief Difference between the First and Second Folios of Shakespeare. Englische Studien, XXX, 1902.

Weber's Selections from the Southern Poets. Mod. Lang. Notes, XVII, 1902.

Does Industrialism Kill Literature? The World's Work, New York, May, 1902.

Literature and Industrialism. Tulane University Record, New Orleans, May 1902; Proceedings of the Conference for Education in the South, 1904.

BIBLIOGRAPHY OF C. ALPHONSO SMITH 187

Why Young Men Should Study Shakespeare. University Society, New York, 1902.
An English-German Conversation Book, in collaboration with Dr. Gustav Krüger, of Berlin. D. C. Heath & Co., Boston, 1902.
Bible Study. University of North Carolina Magazine, December, 1902.
The Novel in America. Teachers' Annuity and Aid Association of the District of Columbia, 1903. Sewanee Review, April, 1904.
Our Language, Third Book, Grammar. B. F. Johnson Publishing Co., Richmond, Va., 1903.
The Publication Department of the Southern Presbyterian Church. Presbyterian Committee of Publication, Richmond, Va., 1904.
The Short Circuit in English Syntax. Mod. Lang. Notes, XIX, 1904.
Memory Work in Literature. School Review, Chicago, XII, 1904.
Life in the Center. University of North Carolina Magazine, March, 1905.
Honor in Student Life in Colleges and Universities. Educational Review, New York, November, 1905.
John Motley Morehead. South Atlantic Quarterly, Durham, N. C., January, 1906.
Studies in English Syntax. Ginn and Company, New York, 1906.
Our Language, Second Book. B. F. Johnson Publishing Co., Richmond, Va., 1906.
Our Debt to Cornelius Harnett. University of North Carolina Magazine, May, 1907.
"You All" as Used in the South. Uncle Remus's Magazine, Atlanta, Ga., July, 1907; The Kit-Kat, Columbus,

Ohio, January, 1920; Southern Review, Asheville, N. C., June, 1920.

Educational Statesmanship in the South. University of North Carolina Record, November, 1907.

The Indicative in an Unreal Condition. Modern Philology, Chicago, January, 1908.

A Bit of News from the Past. University of North Carolina Magazine, May, 1908.

Literature and a Lost Cause. Shurter's Oratory of the South, Neale Publishing Co., Washington, D. C., 1908; Uncle Remus's Magazine, Atlanta, Ga., September, 1909.

Isaac Erwin Avery. Library of Southern Literature, vol. I, Atlanta, Ga., 1908.

Literature in the South. New York Southern Society, 1908; Saxby's Magazine, Cincinnati, Ohio, June, 1909.

The Significance of History in a Democracy. Publications of the North Carolina Historical Commission, Raleigh, 1909.

George Davis. Library of Southern Literature, vol. III, Atlanta, Ga., 1909.

Johnson Jones Hooper. Library of Southern Literature, vol. VI, Atlanta, Ga., 1909.

The Americanism of Poe. Book of the Poe Centenary, University of Virginia, 1909.

Francis Orray Ticknor. Library of Southern Literature, vol. XII, Atlanta, Ga., 1910.

Library of Southern Literature, vol. XIV, Atlanta, Ga., 1910.

Vier Seiten der amerikanischen Literatur (Antrittsrede gehalten am 10. November, 1910, in der Neuen Aula der Berliner Universität): Internationale Wochenschrift, Berlin, November 19, 1910.

BIBLIOGRAPHY OF C. ALPHONSO SMITH 189

The American Short Story. Internationale Wochenschrift, Berlin, December 17, 1910; Ginn and Co., New York, 1912.
Der Charakter der amerikanischen Wohltätigkeit. Die Woche, Berlin, February 11, 1911.
American Literature in Foreign Lands. Louisiana State University Quarterly, Baton Rouge, August, 1911; University of Cincinnati Record, June, 1915.
The Americanism of American Literature. University of North Carolina Record, October, 1911.
Poe as a Constructive Force in World Literature. Old Maryland, Baltimore, November, 1911; University of Virginia Magazine, December, 1911; The Kit-Kat, Columbus, Ohio, April, 1916.
Die amerikanische Literatur (Vorlesungen gehalten an der Königlichen Friedrich-Wilhelms-Universität, B e r l i n : Weidmannche Buchhandlung, Berlin, 1912).
Selections from Huxley. Henry Holt and Co., New York, 1912.
Our Heritage of Idealism. Sewanee Review, April, 1912; Bulletin of the University of South Carolina, July, 1912.
What Should a State History for the Public Schools Contain? North Carolina High School Bulletin, Chapel Hill, April, 1912.
The Negro and the Ballad. University of Virginia Alumni Bulletin, January, 1913.
Dora Duty Jones. Daily Record, Greensboro, N. C., April 3, 1913.
Poe's Mother. Public Ledger, Philadelphia, May 25, 1913.
A National Plea for the Ballad. Bureau of Education, Washington, November, 1913.
Pericles, Prince of Tyre (Tudor Shakespeare). Macmillian Co., New York, 1913.

What Can Literature Do for Me? Doubleday, Page and Company, Garden City, New York, 1913.

English and Scottish Ballads Surviving by Oral Tradition in Virginia. Bulletin of the Virginia Folk-Lore Society, 1913-1921.

Presbyterians in Educational Work in North Carolina Since 1813. Union Seminary Review, Richmond, Va., December-January, 1913-1914.

Inscription on Monument to Nathaniel Greene. Guilford Battleground, near Greensboro, N. C., 1914.

An Appeal to the Teachers of Virginia in Behalf of the Virginia Folk-Lore Society. Department of Public Instruction, Richmond, 1914.

Uncle Henry, Bell-Ringer at the University of Virginia. Corks and Curls, 1914.

O. Henry (Address at the dedication of the O. Henry Memorial, Raleigh, N. C.). Proceedings of the Fifteenth Annual Session of the Literary and Historical Association of North Carolina, Raleigh, 1915; University of Virginia Alumni Bulletin, January, 1915; Sky-Land, Winston-Salem, N. C., March, 1915; Southern Woman's Magazine, Nashville, Tenn., April, 1916.

The Student Body of the University of Virginia. Corks and Curls, 1915; issued in pamphlet form by the University of Virginia, 1915.

Ordinary North-Carolinese. Studies in Philology. Chapel Hill, N. C., April, 1915.

The Link of Literature (a chapter in "America to Japan"). G. P. Putnam's Sons, New York, 1915.

Ballads Surviving in the United States. Musical Quarterly, New York, January, 1916.

A Spelling Test. Virginia High School Bulletin, University, Va., August, 1916.

BIBLIOGRAPHY OF C. ALPHONSO SMITH

Short Stories Old and New. Ginn and Co., New York, 1916.

O. Henry Biography. Doubleday, Page and Co., Garden City, N. Y., 1916.

The Keynote Method. Union Seminary Review, Richmond, Va., October, 1917.

Americanism. Proceedings of the Fiftieth Annual Meeting of the Maryland State Teachers' Association, Baltimore, 1917.

Killis Campbell's Edition of Poe's Poems. Mod. Lang. Notes, March, 1918.

Dialect Writers (a chapter in The Cambridge History of American Literature, vol. II). G. P. Putnam's Sons, New York, 1918.

The Origin of the Pseudonym, O. Henry. The Nation, New York, May 11, 1918; State Journal, Raleigh, N. C., May 31, 1918; Daily News, O. Henry Edition, Greensboro, N. C., July 2, 1919.

Keynote Studies in Keynote Books of the Bible. Fleming H. Revell Co., New York, 1919.

President Graham and the Nation. University of North Carolina Record, Chapel Hill, January, 1919.

William Henry Heck. Virginia Journal of Education, Richmond, Va., March, 1919.

New Words Self-Defined. Doubleday, Page and Co., Garden City, N. Y., 1919.

The Smith-McMurry Language Series, Third Book, Grammar. B. F. Johnson Publishing Co., Richmond, Va., 1919.

Historical Tendencies in Modern Southern Literature. Southern Review, Asheville, N. C., January, 1920.

Poe and the Bible. Biblical Review, New York, July, 1920; University of Virginia Alumni Bulletin, August-October, 1920.

O. Henry a Study in Technique and Personality. Library of Southern Literature, new edition, Atlanta, Ga., 1921.

Edgar Allan Poe: How to Know Him. Bobbs-Merrill Co., Indianapolis, Ind., 1921.

Pinnacle Moments. The Convocation Address delivered in the Amphitheatre, University of Virginia, September 29, 1921. University of Virginia Alumni Bulletin, vol. XIV, No. 4, October, 1921.

The Crisis. Thirty-eighth annual session of the North Carolina Teachers' Assembly, Raleigh, N. C., November, 1921.

Selected Stories from O. Henry. Doubleday, Page and Co., 1922.

Edgar Allan Poe. The Mentor, September, 1922.

O. Henry. The Mentor, February, 1923.

How to Write a Scientific Article. U. S. Naval Academy Proceedings, July, 1923.

Essays on Current Themes. Ginn and Company, 1923.

Matthew Fontaine Maury. University of Virginia Alumni Bulletin, February, 1924.

Literary Contrasts. Ginn and Company, 1925.

www.ingramcontent.com/pod-product-compliance
Lightning Source LLC
Chambersburg PA
CBHW030111010526
44116CB00005B/202